Great
Personal
Statements
for LAW
SCHOOL

Great Personal Statements

for LAW SCHOOL

Paul Bodine
Accepted.com

McGraw-Hill

New York Chicago San Francisco Lisbon London Madrid Mexico City
Milan New Delhi San Juan Seoul Singapore Sydney Toronto

The McGraw·Hill Companies

1 2 3 4 5 6 7 8 9 0   FGR/FGR   0 9 8 7 6 5

ISBN 0-07-145300-8

This publication is designed to provide accurate and authoritative information in regard to the subject matter covered. It is sold with the understanding that neither the author nor the publisher is engaged in rendering legal, accounting, or other professional service. If legal advice or other expert professional assistance is required, the services of a competent professional person should be sought.

—From a Declaration of Principles jointly adopted by a Committee of the American Bar Association and a Committee of Publishers

McGraw-Hill books are available at special quantity discounts to use as premiums and sales promotions, or for use in corporate training programs. For more information, please write to the Director of Special Sales, Professional Publishing, McGraw-Hill, Two Penn Plaza, New York, NY 10121-2298. Or contact your local bookstore.

 This book is printed on recycled, acid-free paper containing a minimum of 50% recycled, de-inked fiber.

For my family

Contents

Acknowledgments

The author would like to extend thanks to Linda Abraham, founder and president of Accepted.com; to Accepted.com's clients; to Accepted.com editors Catherine Cook, Sheila Bender, Cydney Foote, Judy Gruen, Sonia Michaels, Beverly Schneider, and Cindy Tokumitsu; and to Elana Fink.

Special thanks to Jenny Adelman, Bradley Hargis, Victor Roman Dorsey, Jennifer Dunbar, Carl Lammers, Ford O'Connell, M. Ratcliff, Tina Wang, Joe Woloszyn, and Yun-Hee (Oscar) Yang for their invaluable help.

Introduction

The stakes are huge. Newly minted Harvard JDs can earn over $160,000 at the most prestigious big-city firms, with the promise of seven figures if they make partner. And even the median starting salary—$125,000—for graduates of top schools is more than many judges earn. Income is hardly the only measure of a JD's success, of course. A law degree from a top school is now often essential for public-spirited graduates seeking to lead major not-for-profit organizations. Indeed, lawyers are the single largest professional group by far in the U.S. Congress. The message is clear. A JD is a powerful qualification for opening the doors of opportunity, whether you want to change your career or the world.

For law school applicants like you, such rosy prospects create incentive, to be sure, but also an understandable anxiety to execute the law school application well. While it remains true that your undergraduate grades and LSAT scores will play a huge role in deciding your fate, top law schools today know they'll have their pick of applicants with stellar numbers. For that reason, they can afford to look beyond "the numbers" in crafting an optimal class of well-rounded variety. And when admissions committees must choose between equally qualified super-achievers, nothing helps them decide better than your own words.

Enter the personal statement. More than ever, the one to three essays law schools typically invite you to write play the central role in enabling admissions officers see you as a unique person deserving of admission, rather than a lifeless statistical "profile." In searching for help to write these mission-critical documents, you will need more than one-size-fits-all "good writing" tips and a stack of sample essays you wish you'd written. You will need market-tested admissions strategies for crafting essays that communicate the special qualities and insights that will make your story too compelling for admissions professionals to ignore. I've written *Great Personal Statements for Law School* to give you just that. Whether you are a confident writer or not, whether you're applying from college with a traditional law-school-related major, or if you are a card-carrying "nontraditional" applicant, the concrete, practical advice in this book will show you the key "tricks of trade" that have worked consistently for dozens of accepted applicants at law schools like Harvard, New York University, Virginia, Northwestern, Cornell, Duke, Georgetown, and UCLA, among many others.

Great Personal Statements for Law School is the only how-to admissions writing guide to offer the following combination of features:

- Proprietary admissions and writing insights of Accepted.com, one of the oldest and most successful admissions consulting services, whose editors have helped thousands of applicants gain admission to the world's best professional schools since 1994. As the senior editor at Accepted.com since 1997, I've distilled into this book almost 10 years of personal experience advising successful applicants from every demographic and region of the world (a sample of my clients' testimonials can be found on Accepted.com's Web site at www.accepted.com/aboutus/EditorTestimonials.aspx?EditorID=2)

- A flexible, practical system for finding your application's self-marketing handle; brainstorming your essays' raw material using six "data-mining" techniques; crafting an outline using theme and evidence sentences; and writing, revising, and editing effective essay drafts

- Detailed strategies for answering the most common law school essay topics: diversity and obstacles overcome; accomplishments, strengths, and interests; and why law school

- Practical guidelines for understanding what schools actually ask (based on analysis of the top 70 law programs' applications) and choosing appropriate stories for each essay type

- More than 30 actual, complete essays or admissions documents written by admitted applicants to law schools like the University of Chicago, Georgetown, Cornell, Virginia, and Indiana, including such specialized admissions documents as outlines, diversity statements, addenda, letters of recommendation, and transfer essays

- Specific treatment of such special admissions topics as customizing essays to particular schools, handling public-interest career goals, waging a guerilla wait-list campaign, submitting "value-added" deans' letters, crafting effective addenda, and educating your recommenders

Chapter 1 of *Great Personal Statements for Law School* guides you through the hardest part of the application process—actually writing the essays—by showing you how to:

- Create a self-marketing handle that informs your whole application

- Drill down to the themes and stories on which your essays will be built

- Use outlines effectively

- Approach the first draft and revision/editing stages confidently

In Chapter 2, you learn what schools look for in the personal statement as well as practical strategies for writing on the most common topics: diversity and personal challenge; accomplishments, strengths, and interests; and why the law. In Chapter 3, we consider the secondary essay in all its varieties, from required secondary essays and optional essays with defined topics to open-ended optional essays and addenda. We close the chapter with a detailed plan for getting off the wait list. In Chapter 4, we'll tell you the most effective strategies for selecting and approaching recommenders and give you detailed advice for tackling the most common recommendation topics: your intellectual skills, your writing skills, and your character. The last section of the book contains 30 actual personal statements and related admissions documents that helped real applicants gain admission to law school.

Great Personal Statements for Law School is designed to benefit motivated, conscientious applicants to the world's leading law schools who need a no-nonsense, thoroughly road-tested guide to admissions writing. We cannot promise, of course, that following the advice in these pages will assure you admission. "Magic bullets" or rigid systems cannot guarantee you success in a process that is so inherently complex and personal. There are many different ways to approach and write your essays, and we encourage you to use the advice that helps you and modify or ignore the rest.

I wrote this book with the assumption that effective admissions writing involves much more than just reading other applicants' essays or trying to figure out what admissions officers want to hear. Good writing is about uncovering and polishing the special blend of skills, experiences, and values that only you possess. It demands self-understanding, honesty, analysis, and hard work. I have yet to meet a client who didn't have a unique story to tell. You have one too. Helping you find it is why so many of my clients have the degrees they dreamed of.

A NOTE ON THE SAMPLE DOCUMENTS

All the essays reproduced in this book are real essays—not composites or ideal models—written by actual applicants from a wide range of backgrounds who were admitted by the law school listed before each sample. To protect these applicants' privacy, personal details like gender and cultural background, proper names, and other nonessential details have sometimes been disguised.

It goes without saying that it is both illegal and unethical to copy or adapt any of these samples for use in your own application.

The author welcomes any input for improving later editions of this book. Contact Paul Bodine at pbodine@accepted.com.

1

Getting Started

"Another book on writing law school personal statements? But everyone knows getting into law school is 90 percent LSAT and GPA and 10 percent luck! Why bother?" You've probably heard, perhaps even shared, the conventional wisdom about the law school application game. You know that law schools live and die by their rankings and that those rankings are heavily weighted toward applicants' performance in four years of college and four hours of standardized testing. You know, in other words, that before you even think about writing your personal statement, the list of schools you can get into may already be limited. You may also know that at some schools "preferred applicant" programs even drop the essay requirement altogether for applicants with killer numbers.

Unfortunately, if you were planning to use any of these facts as an excuse for phoning in a half-baked personal statement, you'd be playing Russian roulette with your admission hopes. Nothing is as simple as it sounds, and that includes the bromide that "law school admissions is all LSAT and GPA." Even for numbers-obsessed law schools (and, in some respects, especially for them), the personal statement can be a deal breaker or deal maker.

Don't believe me? Consider this: in 2004 Yale Law admitted only 45 percent of applicants who posted LSATs of 175 *and* GPAs of 3.75 or above—nearly half, that is, of the best of the very best, numerically speaking. Why were so many "perfect" applicants shown the door? The reasons, no doubt, varied. But because, for admissions officials ("adcoms" for short), the personal statement is the primary tool for understanding your nonnumerical profile, you can bet that bad essays were the culprit in sabotaging many of these numerically flawless applications.

But reading the tea leaves of admissions statistics isn't the only clue to the personal statement's importance. You can ask the adcoms themselves. No less than Harvard's assistant admissions dean has been quoted as saying "A personal statement is often a make-or-break component of an application," and the vast majority of remaining adcoms are just as emphatic. Adcoms for schools as diverse as Boalt Hall and George Washington are also on record as admitting that personal statements carry the same weight as the vaunted LSAT and GPA.

Then there's the circumstantial evidence. Many law school applicants have reported notes, phone calls, or personal comments from adcoms praising them for personal statements that clearly won them admission. Or consider that, unlike business schools, few law schools conduct interviews to learn about their applicants. Where can adcoms look to gain some sense of the person? Only the essays can fill that role. And while business schools invite applicants to write several essays, most law schools offer you only one personal statement and, if you're lucky, an optional essay to show the real you. The burden the personal statement carries in showing adcoms the person behind the numbers could hardly be greater.

It is true that most schools will use your LSAT score and GPA to do an initial sort of their applications. Thus, some applicants, the so-called presumptive admits, will have a leg up on the competition and others, the "presumptive denies," will find themselves in a hole they must climb out of before their essays have even been seen. But *presumptive* doesn't necessarily mean "automatic," and most applicants won't be labeled presumptive anything. They'll have to duke it out with their peers in a competitive ring where "the numbers" may have been their ticket in, but the qualitative aspect—that is, the personal statement—decides the match.

For years, many law admissions experts have echoed the "only numbers count" line, though the exceptions they noted—the applicants for whom personal statements really *do* matter—make an interesting collection:

- *Applicants to top schools.* Their LSATs and GPAs are so uniformly high that the personal statement becomes the adcoms' key tool for distinguishing among them.

- *Applicants from underrepresented minority groups.* Since Supreme Court decisions have forced many big state schools to abandon separate "indexes" (LSAT–GPA weighting formulas) for minority and nonminority applicants, adcoms must look more closely at the non-numerical parts of their applications (read: essays) to identify reasons to bring these applicants aboard.

■ *Applicants at schools in any tier who fall into the large middle pool of applicants.* If you are not a presumptive admit or a presumptive deny, your LSAT and GPA are too close to your competitors' to play a decisive role in your admission decision. By throwing you in the middle of the pack, adcoms are saying that they need more information than your numbers have provided. Your essays are a main source of that information.

■ *Applicants who are vying for the last spots in a class.* With the vast majority of admission offers already made, law schools probably won't be able to improve their next-year rankings by rounding out their class with more high LSAT or GPA types. More likely, they'll be looking to tweak the class's "diversity" profile by scouting applications for unusual backgrounds, experiences, or hobbies. Guess where they expect to learn about those? In your personal statement.

■ *Applicants who have truly unusual experiences.* The applicant who has overcome a brutal childhood of neglect and abuse to graduate from Harvard on scholarship, the candidate who led a labor movement in his home country before coming to the United States to earn the law degree that will help him run for office back home, the applicant who won two book awards and taught English in south central Los Angeles—truly exceptional candidates convince adcoms to overlook uncompetitive numbers through their essays.

■ *Applicants applying to law schools that evaluate applications without index-based screens or cutoffs.* Some schools have no index-driven applicant ranking system and give every applicant, they claim, the same full review, with no specific weight given to any one factor in the application. For these schools, the weight your essay carries in determining your fate is magnified.

■ *Applicants who are "mixed predictors."* If you have either a high LSAT and a low GPA or a low LSAT and a high GPA, you probably have a hunch where the adcoms look to decide whether to ignore your low number or ding (reject) you with it: you've got it, your personal statement.

■ *Applicants applying to "safety" schools.* Since these applicants' numbers are strong enough to earn them admission by themselves, adcoms won't read their essays to locate positive information (they have all they need). Instead, they'll be read "negatively"—to see if you've given them a reason to ding you despite your great numbers.

■ *Applicants applying to lower-tier schools who have unimpressive numbers.* This is the mirror image of the dilemma the tier-one schools face: how do you distinguish between applicants whose numbers are uniformly *unimpressive*? You look more closely at the qualitative—the personal statement.

Add up all these "exceptions" to the only-numbers-matter rule and you'll find precious few applicants for whom the essay *doesn't* matter in an absolutely mission-critical way. Whoever you are, a good personal statement probably plays a pivotal role in your admissions chances.

When applicants' test scores and grades, recommendations, work experience, and extracurriculars are all uniformly superlative, law adcoms could make admissions decisions with a coin flip. How much fairer is it that they instead take the time to let applicants' thoughts about their lives, dreams, and accomplishments influence their decisions? To put it another way, law schools are actually doing you a favor by giving your essays so much weight. How so? Because, of all the components of your application, the personal statement is the one over which you have the greatest control. Your LSAT scores and grades are now history, your recommenders may or may not say what you want them to say, and even if your school offers an admissions interview, its success depends on such external factors as your interviewer's questions and mood.

But your personal statement is all yours. From the themes you choose to capture your unique profile and the stories you pick to illustrate them to the lessons you draw and the tone you adopt, law schools give you the reins to shape their perception of your candidacy.

KNOW THY AUDIENCE

Any successful piece of writing begins with assessing its intended audience. Writing is really just a means of striking up a certain kind of personal relationship with the reader, and who you think that reader is obviously affects what you say to him or her.

Too many applicants doom their essays from the start by assuming they're addressing the educational equivalent of a parole board. The essays of unsuccessful applicants often read like they were written for an audience of rubber-stamping, degree-issuing automatons or surly Dickensian gatekeepers waiting to pounce on signs of individuality. The essays of successful applicants, in contrast, recognize that their readers are real people with specific backgrounds and expectations. The road to becoming a successful applicant starts with being savvy about exactly who is on the receiving end of your application.

There are three basic types of admissions readers: professional admissions officers, law professors, and students. While professors and students may not ever read your application, depending on the school and your place in the applicant pool, you can be dead certain that admissions officers will. No matter where you apply or with what numbers, an admissions officer will review your application, even if only to decide that your numbers are too low to merit a closer look. Adcoms are your core audience.

If you find any pattern in the background of typical adcom members, it will be that of the lifelong admissions careerist—that is, professionals (often women) with human resource–oriented degrees who've worked their way through the admissions food chain, often at several schools. Increasingly, they have law degrees from the schools they serve, though this is still the exception. Instead of statisticians, number-crunchers, or demographic analysts, in other words, you'll find HR, marketing, and lawyer types or eclectic multi-careerists (such as the financial aid specialist, the career counselor or placement expert, or the part-time reader who reads applications on a contract basis).

What does all this tell you? That your essay will be read by qualitatively oriented "people persons" with varied backgrounds and interests *who value this same profile in applicants.* On some level, then, you want your application to communicate that you too are a people person and not a "noncontributory," a well-rounded eclectic type and not a dronish library-dweller.

But you must also keep in mind your secondary audience: law professors. At most schools, law professors enter the picture after the adcoms have made the first general decisions or "sortings" of the applicant pool and now seek confirmation of their first calls and help in making the tougher ones. At some schools, the professor-reader is one of the law school's legal writing faculty, and your personal statement will be scrutinized for signs of a facile command of language. As a general rule, the smaller the class size of the school, the larger the role professors are likely to play in reviewing files. The odds then are that your application will be read by a law professor.

Law professors are, first and last, smart. They had to be the best at their law schools to earn the chance to teach law as a career, so you can assume that many of them were on law review or clerked for a judge. You can assume, in other words, that they have high standards (low tolerance for mediocrity), strong ambitions (and sympathy for others who do too), focused personalities (an admiration for determination in others), and unusually critical minds (and thus impatience with superficial or sloppy thinking, poor writing, and an inability to balance ambiguous or contradictory ideas).

Finally, law professors are also lawyers, which means they are gatekeepers not only for the school but for the entire profession. They want to see that you have thought about what commitment to a law career means (*not* that you know how to sling legal lingo around). Unlike the adcom, the law professor usually views reading applications as a minor part of his or her real job— teaching, researching, and consulting—a fact you'll want to remember when you're debating whether to spend more time on your essays to eliminate mistakes, wordiness, and uninteresting material.

At many schools, student readers bring up the rear. As survivors of the ordeal you seek to inflict on yourself, they will have the least patience for naiveté and ill-informed assumptions about law school. As your near peers, they will have the most acute sense of your potential fit or lack of it in the school's student culture. If law professors will be judging you on the quality of your mind, student readers will be judging you on the quality of your personality. Would they really want to face your charming self day after day through the most grueling experience of their lives? Your goal is to make them answer, "Yes."

How does one craft a single essay that addresses each of these reader types? First, realize that pleasing the adcoms and student readers by being interesting and personable while also pleasing the professors by showing purpose, intelligence, and verbal skills are hardly mutually exclusive goals. You can do both within a single essay without seeming schizophrenic; this book will show you how. Second, remember that, in the overwhelming number of cases, the law professors on admissions committees agree with the initial recommendations of the adcoms—more than 90 percent of the time. Adcoms and professors may be playing different instruments, but they're all reading from the same score: create a class that's capable, but also personally compelling.

THE ADMISSIONS PARTY

Imagine you're at a tony cocktail party where you find yourself competing with the best and brightest of your peers to make a lasting impression on your welcoming but overworked hosts. You're all splendidly accomplished, well-rounded types, but you know your influential hosts are only likely to remember a handful of you when the evening's done. When your moment comes, will you collar them and begin reciting your academic or professional feats? Let's hope not.

You'd probably turn on the charm, complimenting them on their home, probing for areas of shared interest, telling a few of your choice stories, and generally captivating them with your engaging personality. On one level, your law school essays represent this same interpersonal challenge: how to put your best foot forward when your personal distinctiveness, no longer your LSAT score and grades, is what will separate you from the other super achievers vying for your law school spot. If there are three applicant categories—the dings, the "doables," and the dazzling—it's in your personal statement and essays that you can elevate yourself from the doable to the dazzling.

FINDING YOUR SELF-MARKETING HANDLE

The essay-writing process begins with introspection; there's no shortcut around it. Before you begin writing, you should develop a short personal marketing message or "handle" that integrates the key themes (strengths, experiences, interests) you want your application to communicate. Picture our admissions cocktail party again. Your hosts' time is limited. They must make the rounds with all their guests before the night is over. Since you can't give them your whole life story, everything you say must communicate a compact multidimensional message that's distinctive enough for your hosts to remember long after other partygoers have made their pitch. Take your time, cast your net widely, and ask friends and family for their input, so that the handle you devise reflects the key uniqueness factors from your personal, professional, academic, and community lives.

As a rule of thumb, aim for a self-marketing handle comprised of two or three themes. If you come up with "A natural writer with strong analytical skills and a social conscience," you're thinking a bit too broadly. Likewise, if your handle runs past a sentence or two, unless it's truly scintillating, law schools may garble it or lose it in the crowd. The blend of themes should emphasize your multi-dimensionality. That is, you're not only an honors student in history at Brown, but *also* a Norwegian American raised in Ecuador who *also* loves making documentaries and tutoring immigrant kids for Knowledge Trust Alliance.

Remember that your admissions "hosts" will be bringing a long memory of past conversations to your brief encounter. Simply telling them you're a paralegal or a poli-sci major will trigger all sorts of (valid) assumptions about your skills and professional exposures. If you're applying from a traditional law school major like political science or history, for example, your handle will come equipped with some analytical or verbal strengths. So round it out distinctively by including themes that law schools don't automatically associate with your profile, such as creativity (e.g., your lifelong devotion to writing poetry), social impact causes (e.g., that summer you trained subsistence farmers in Malawi), or out-of-the-box professional experiences (e.g., your post-college career as a geography teacher). Or look for unusual childhood or family experiences, distinctive hobbies, or international experiences that offset the predictability of your profile—and then incorporate these in your handle.

Conversely, if your profile is unusual (e.g., creative or highly international) law schools will already be giving you points for distinctiveness, so balance your handle with themes that show them that you also have the analytical, writing, or research skills they automatically associate with history and philosophy majors. Instead of "The award-winning African American photographer who grew up in Portugal and sings in her church's choir," pitch yourself as "The Lisbon-raised African American photographer who wrote a successful guide to digital nature photography and handles her church's finances." Like the traditional applicant, your goal is a self-marketing handle that communicates interesting well-roundedness, but you achieve it by reassuring schools that you're law school caliber—in addition to being unlike anyone they've encountered before.

Your search for your application's self-marketing handle will inevitably involve some comparison with other applicants. Relying only on your own sense of your distinctive strengths may not be enough to separate you from your peers, especially if you're a member of a crowded applicant demographic. For example, a nonminority political science major from the University of Illinois with work experience as a paralegal could be forgiven for deciding that the strongest aspects of his profile are his 170 LSAT score and 3.7 GPA at a selective public university. Unfortunately, at the top-10 law schools his background will only be par for the course (at best). To find a self-marketing handle that really sets him apart, he'll have to dig deeper—perhaps by focusing on unusual aspects of his upbringing (obstacles overcome, for example, or unusual international experience) or hobbies or involvements that few of his peers will share. You can use law schools' class profiles to gain a sense of the educational, ethnic, geographic, and professional backgrounds of past matriculants. Experienced admissions consultants such as Accepted.com can also help you isolate the potential themes that could make your handle stand out.

Although a distinctive multidimensional handle is ideal, it must truly capture who you are. Don't try to force a theme—"internationalism," for example, or "creativity"—onto your profile if you don't have the experiences to back it up. Be real.

DATA-MINING YOUR LIFE

Once you have your self-marketing handle, you have the multipart message that should inform your personal statement and essays for every school. Now you need to find the best *specific* story or stories to illustrate that message. Unlike business schools, which help you by posing several highly specific "thesis-bearing" essay topics—topics, that is, whose theme is contained in the wording of the question itself—law schools often give you carte blanche in formulating your personal statement's subject matter. Michigan, for example, bluntly states "The topic of the personal statement is entirely up to you," and Harvard is no more helpful: "It is for you to decide what information you would like to convey and the best way for you to convey it." This may feel like cruel and unusual punishment when you're writing, but look on the bright side. By being so open-ended, schools are actually giving you the freedom to blow them away with a well-executed essay about what *really* matters to you. Take advantage of it.

Study the wording of the personal statement instructions carefully. For all the expressive freedom they give you, most schools offer quite a few hints as to the kinds of material they hope to read about. For example, right after declaring "The subject matter of your personal statement is up to you," Utah helpfully prompts you with "What background, experiences, and events (positive or negative) have affected you? What perspectives and experiences might you bring to classroom discussions and the law school community? What are your motivations for seeking a legal education?" You can safely conclude that an effective essay will encompass one (or more) of these topics.

Before writing, reflect on these kinds of subject-matter prompts for a week or so to get your mind working on them in background mode. You will hear a lot (in this book too) about "positioning" themes and thinking "strategically" about your essays, but none of that will make any difference if you don't first respond in an honest, self-revealing way to the invitation the personal statement extends to you. After all your savvy positioning, some of that sincerity must shine through or your essays will read as blandly as a committee-written Hollywood script.

Now you're ready to identify the individual story or stories you will build your essays around.

Mind-Plumbing Methods

The data-mining or "life inventory" step is nonoptional. You should no more exclude it from the essay-writing process than you would omit rehearsing a piece of music before performing it publicly, or conducting research before writing a thesis. It's that essential. Inventorying your own life is by definition a subjective process. Your memory can deceive you, stories you consider unexceptional may actually make an outstanding essay, and tales that you're convinced are distinctive and impressive may actually be fairly commonplace. So at this early stage you want to suspend judgment and simply "brain-dump" as much as you can as quickly as you can. The goal here is to find different ways to bypass your inhibitions and trick your mind into disgorging details you overlooked, significant events you've taken for granted, passions you forgot you once had.

Several techniques may help you:

■ *Visual mapping or clustering.* Write the two or three themes that constitute your self-marketing handle on separate sheets of paper. Around each of your theme words begin jotting down whatever events, skills, values, or interests these words suggest to you. Each new term you jot down will suggest other words. Follow them where they lead, and connect each new term with a line back to the related term that prompted it. If you go with the flow here you may gain insights into what you value most and the inter-connections between your themes. All of these may prove useful when you begin writing your personal statement and essays.

■ *Using your résumé as an autobiographical time line.* Your résumé can be a memory aid for generating essay material. Let your mind linger over each section of the résumé, recalling the challenges, breakthroughs, and changes each stage of your career has offered you. Recall and write down the full details of the accomplishments listed in the résumé's bullets, as well as the achievements you had to exclude from the résumé that might also make good essay fodder. Since your personal statement may involve a chronologically ordered narrative, this exercise can generate useful material and a timeframe for understanding your development.

■ *Random listing.* Instead of shackling your thought to the rules of sentences and paragraphs, first warm up your writing skills by generating simple lists—favorite music; worst jobs or classes; greatest accomplishments; best vacations; traits that define you; characteristics your friends admire in you; or the most unusual things about your childhood, education, international travels, hobbies, and so on. Then take these lists a step further by looking for any connections between them. For example, perhaps your list of defining traits is illustrated by your list of achievements.

■ *Recording thoughts or conversations.* If you are one of those people who find any kind of writing exercise inhibiting, a digital voice or tape recorder may enable you to get your thoughts out. Either record yourself as you extemporize about your life or goals or record a conversation with a friend as he or she probes you with some basic "life" questions like these:

- What makes you happiest?
- Think about the last article you read that made you feel really angry or inspired. What was it about and why did you react so strongly to it?
- What one person influenced you more than anyone else in your life? In what ways?
- What would your friends be most surprised to learn about you?
- If you could choose your epitaph, what would it say and why?
- What single event changed your life or your values the most, positively or negatively?
- What has been your greatest failure and what did you learn from it?
- If you could be any person living or dead besides yourself, who would it be? Why?

Transcribe this recording (minus the "um"s and "like"s), and you'll have a rough but potentially useful data bank of essay content.

■ *Stream-of-consciousness writing.* Perhaps the least structured of techniques, stream-of-consciousness or "free" writing simply involves scribbling down whatever comes into your head without stopping, even if it's nonsense. As odd as this may sound, you'll find that for all the useless verbiage you generate, you'll also unwittingly produce ideas, phrases, and insights that may actually wind up in your essays. Try to group these ideas, phrases, and insights into related bundles. At a minimum, this technique can help you overcome the angst of the empty page.

■ *Journaling.* Nothing will get you into the discipline of writing better than a daily regimen. The operative word here is *daily*—anything less frequent will prevent you from writing naturally and unselfconsciously. Pick a time of day when you can write uninterruptedly for 15 minutes to a half hour. Record your thoughts, dreams, experiences of the past day, whatever you want, but do it without fail and without distractions. Avoid the trap of simply recording your comings and goings, however. Make it a practice to close each paragraph by drawing some conclusion or stating its significance. Writing thoughtfully is a habit you can learn.

What do all these exercises have in common? They get you writing *before* you begin writing your personal statement, when anxiety and your "internal editor" can cut you off from the creativity and personality that will make your essays live. The mere act of translating your thoughts into words—in whatever form—forces those thoughts to the next level of concreteness and leads you in new directions, while also giving you a paper trail to refer back to as raw material for your personal statement. Writing, in other words, is a way of thinking, a kind of introspection. The sooner you get into the habit of thinking on paper (or screen), the sooner you'll be ready to shape that thinking into the rigorous, ordered thought that is the essay. Crossing the great divide between your thoughts and their verbal expression in concrete language is what separates would-be writers from nonwriters. It's not easy, but these exercises can help you do it with a minimum of pain.

Everything Signifies

Your data-mining or "life inventory" process should involve more then merely flushing out the stories that best capture your self-marketing themes. You also want to be continually evaluating their significance. How valuable was that congressional internship to me? What did it teach me, or how did it change me? To manage your data-mining effort, create a spreadsheet or log divided into sections—say, Academics, Jobs, Extracurriculars, Community/Volunteering, and Personal/Family. Within each section create three columns: one for describing the event, one for noting its "external" significance or impact, and a third for logging its "internal" significance to you. External significance will include the experience's impact on your career or academic progress (earned honors or promotion, etc.), on your organization (raised $5,000 for fraternity, won new client contract), or on others (helped tutoring student raise math grade to B). Internal significance will include how the experience changed you, enhanced your skills, deepened your perspective, strengthened your sense of your potential, and so on.

By getting into the habit of identifying and jotting down the underlying significance of your stories as they come to you, you'll sharpen your ability to evaluate your essay material in the same way that admissions officers will, thus reducing your burden in the essay-writing stage.

Don't perform the critical data-mining stage all by yourself. Your perception of your own life is likely to be highly subjective, so ask friends, family, and mentors for any key traits, memories, accomplishments you may have missed.

From Raw Material to Essay Content

If you've done it right, your data-mining process should leave you with a mass of raw material that could fill several personal statements. As much as you may want to throw it all into the pot, essay length limits will force you to jettison the bulk of it. So get used to thinking early on in terms of focused stories or experiences that capture in microcosm what's essential about you rather than "overview" essays that superficially skim dozens of key moments. These latter essays usually come off as glorified lists that lack the detail and context that enable readers to remember your stories, and hence you. Look for discrete stories that can "stand in for" or serve as metaphors for your life's themes. By understanding these stories, in other words, someone could know nearly as much about who you really are as by hearing your full autobiography. Given the limited space that law schools give you, you will only be able to suggest the breadth of your life experiences by exploring a key handful in depth.

Because you approached the data-mining stage with your self-marketing handle already defined, you were able to group your raw stories or data points into buckets that corresponded to the handle's two or three themes. Your data-mining process may have shown you that your handle was overemphasizing one aspect of your profile or ignoring one that you now think is stronger. Be flexible; make whatever adjustments you need to.

Now begin to evaluate your raw stories critically. Look for the ones that are most distinctive and that combine the greatest external impact and personal transformation. If a story is scoring high in (1) unusualness, (2) objective results or impact, and (3) personal significance to you, you've probably got a winner. How well does this story illustrate your theme? Katie has three possible stories to illustrate her "internationalism" theme: the five years she lived in Zanzibar as a tyke, a college internship in Thailand, and her senior thesis on labor movements in the Baltic states. She has other stories she wants to tell, so she decides she can't discuss all *three* of these. Which one should she narrate in full? Which should she just mention in passing? As a general rule, more recent stories trump older ones, and life experiences beat academic ones. However, the depth of the impact of the experience on you is your surest guide. Weighing her choices, Katie decides to focus on the Thailand internship. (Good choice.)

Subject all the raw stories generated by this data-mining process to this same weighing or ranking process until you've arrived at a core set of stories that you want your personal statement and essays to tell. Now—at last—you're ready to actually start telling them.

WRITING YOUR PERSONAL STATEMENT

Because you performed the content-gathering steps in the last section, now that you're beginning your personal statement you should not only know which stories you want to use but also have done enough raw writing to avoid "blank page syndrome" and related writers' ailments. Still, writing tends to bring out the procrastinator in all of us, so set tight deadlines of a few days or less for completing each stage of your statement. As in the data-mining process, your focus when writing the first draft is just to get something down on paper. Many applicants believe they have to complete a polished, finished draft in one sitting. Don't be so hard on yourself. Good writing is not about home runs; it's a base-at-a-time game. So forget about style, grammar, and word count when writing your first draft.

To keep the pressure off, start with the first application that comes out in the summer or with a school that's not your number one choice. After you finish it, move on to the next school, but don't submit the first application. After you finish the second or third school's application (and perhaps others), go back to the first school and polish it off in light of the tweaks you've made while working on later applications. In this way you can capitalize on the improvements that inevitably occur as you refine your personal statement without jeopardizing the advantage of applying early.

The Outline Is Your Friend

Not to be confused with the case outline dear to the hearts of every first-year law student, the academic-style outline provides a useful method for reducing the anxiety and time drain of the writing process. If outlines make you nervous or stifle your creative juices, you *can* develop your essays in unstructured fashion by simply expanding the raw content you generated in the data-mining process into larger chunks or paragraphs, and then juggling their order until you find one that fits. The (substantial) downside of this approach is its hap-hazardness and inefficiency. By failing to map out your essay's organization from the start, you risk chasing tangents down blind alleys, wasting valuable time.

By bringing structure to your essay before you start writing it, outlines maximize your efficiency and enable you to perform a crucial early test of your essay ideas before you've invested too much in them. Do you have enough material to support your assertions or illustrate your experiences? Does the lesson you're trying to draw from your material have enough substance? Does it really grow organically from the story itself or does it seem imposed and unearned? Outlines can help you answer these questions.

Each outline you create will have the following basic organization:

1. *Introduction.* One paragraph introducing the essay's themes and setting its tone. For example, in the actual applicant outline shown as sample 1 in the Sample Documents section at the end of this book, the introduction uses a vivid image of a Dentist from Hell, which simultaneously grabs the reader's attention and introduces the incident that motivates the applicant to seek a law career.

2. *Body paragraphs.* Anywhere from two to three or more paragraphs that provide evidence to support the themes asserted in the introduction. In law school you may learn the "IRAC" model for tackling law school exams: State the (I)ssue, state the (R)ule that applied, (A)pply the rule to the facts, and state your (C)onclusion. In that spirit of acronym, we here offer the TELL model for tackling law school personal statements: State the (T)heme sentence, back it up with a story or (E)xample, then state the (L)esson (L)earned from the story. Following this, each paragraph in the body should consist of:

   a. *Theme sentence.* The first sentence of the paragraph states the topic or theme that this paragraph will "prove": "Though my family tree says 'Old South,' all my instincts are New England."

   b. *Evidence sentences.* These consist of specific examples, anecdotes, or detail that support the paragraph's theme sentence. "In my very first project, for example, I performed the research on and wrote the first draft for a brownfields bill that was later passed by the Georgia legislature."

3. *Conclusion.* This paragraph pulls together the underlying lessons or themes of the preceding paragraphs. It generally includes lessons learned or insights (from the third column of your data-mining spreadsheet): "I learned that sometimes the best way to find out who you really are is to screw up." Note how the author of the outline in sample 1 uses his conclusion to refer ahead to law school and refer back to the Nazi dentist image that opened the essay.

A good outline is the safety rope that keeps you focused on finding that next secure foothold toward your essay's summit rather than staring dizzily into the abyss of an empty paragraph. Don't cling to your outline cravenly, however. It may need to be revised as your thinking about the topic evolves.

The First Draft

According to writing coach Elizabeth Danziger, you should devote no more than 15 percent of your total time on writing the first draft (with the remaining time divided between the brainstorming and revising steps). Whether that number is accurate or not, the moral is that writing your first draft should not paralyze you with anxiety or perfectionism. You've already done a major portion of your work (finding, selecting, and structuring your material), and the bulk of your remaining work (revision and editing) comes later. So lighten up! Run with your outline, and don't analyze what you're writing too closely—just get it down.

Some writers start with the sections of the outline that look easiest or that they know the most about. And for many writers, the introduction is often the last piece of the puzzle. In the next three sections, however, we'll look at the three main components of every essay—the introduction, body, and conclusion—in that order.

Introduction

One traditional purpose of the introduction is to tell the reader what you will be trying to accomplish in the personal statement. This does not mean that your first sentence should be a monotonous statement of your theme ("In this essay, I will . . ."), but somewhere in your first paragraph you should signal what the overriding message of your essay will be.

More than stating your theme, however, your introduction must catch and hold the reader's interest, which is battered daily by dozens of same-sounding essays. (Some adcoms read 50 or more essays a day—imagine.) Given that adcoms only have time to focus 8 to 10 minutes on your application (that's right, your *application*, not just your essay), it's critical that they finish your introduction thinking "How will this turn out?" or "Hmmm, interesting . . ." rather than "Here we go again." Finally, to help your reader find his or her bearings, your introduction should also provide some of the essay's key context (answering Where? When? Who? and What?) and establish, primarily through word choice, the essay's tone (for example, dramatic and serious, or wry and subtle).

Body

The body of your essay is also its heart—the human story and the corroborating "evidence" that justifies the claims or promises you make (explicitly or implicitly) in your introduction. Every paragraph in the body should be built on a basic pattern of *general assertion → supporting example*. That is, whether you're writing a narrative-driven chronological essay, an example-driven "argument" essay, or a vivid detail-driven descriptive essay, every paragraph should begin with a general-focus *theme sentence* and then several sentences of specific-focus *evidence sentences*—anecdotes, examples, descriptions, or actions—that illustrate the theme sentence.

Each paragraph in the body should advance your "case" or further unfold your story. Usually, the specific sequence of your paragraphs will be dictated by the chronology of the story you're telling (from the past toward the present), but sometimes, as in an essay about your strengths, each paragraph will function as a separate example in a larger argument. In either case, your paragraphs will live or die by the degree of personal, vivid detail and insight you provide. You want to achieve a balance between "data"—the personal facts and stories that substantiate your themes—and analysis—regularly stepping back from an example or anecdote to tell the reader what it means. Too much data will make for a dull, impersonal essay. Too much analysis will cause your personal statement to float off into a sea of generalities unsupported by anchoring facts.

Perhaps the greatest disadvantage you face as an applicant is that you cannot read what the vast majority of other applicants write. If you could, you would instantly see how many essays sound the same! The reason for this interchangeability is almost always a lack of specific detail and personal anecdote. So throughout the body of your essay, always be as personal and specific as you can.

You know your personal statement's body is structured well when the opening theme sentences connecting each new paragraph to the preceding (called *transition sentences*) seem to write themselves. For example, the transition sentence, "The Marziello case was not the last time I took on responsibilities beyond my job description," smoothly links the preceding paragraph (about the Marziello case) to another leadership example the writer is about to narrate in the new paragraph. Try to avoid graceless transitions that rely on numbers—"Third, the law for me means the rule of order in a chaotic and arbitrary universe."

Conclusion

Your conclusion needs to do several key things—and briefly. It needs to draw a synthesized (but not vague or banal) lesson or theme out of the body paragraphs that have preceded it. And it must do so without simply repeating the theme statement from the introduction or merely restating the key point of each body paragraph. The conclusion must create a true sense of "summing up"—of loose ends being bow-tied—but in a way that injects deeper or larger insight than was previously provided in the personal statement. Moreover, to give the reader that peculiar feeling of coherence or unity that good writing often has, your conclusion should refer indirectly back to the language or details of the introduction—but as an indirect echo rather than a mirror. Finally, the conclusion's tone must be positive and forward-looking. If it makes sense in context to refer to your goals or law school plans, do so, but don't force it just because you think it's de rigueur. Avoid "In conclusion," or any of its stuffy siblings.

As you work on your first draft, keep your outline in front of you so you don't wander off into tedious digressions. If you start to feel lost or bogged down, pull back and ask yourself "What am I really trying to say here?" "What do I want the reader to feel, believe, or conclude after reading this?" These kinds of reorienting exercises can keep you on track and plowing speedily toward your immediate objective: a reasonably coherent document within which lurks a finalized personal statement.

If it helps, try to think of your personal statement not as an argument ("Why I should be admitted") or a proposal ("Consider admitting me for the following reasons") but as a story about an interesting and sympathetic hero (you) in pursuit of a distant but most holy grail (the JD). Humans are hardwired to respond to human-interest stories. Tales of sympathetic protagonists overcoming conflict or obstacles by modifying their world to remove those obstacles appeal to our basic hopes in a way that impersonal proposals do not. This is not to suggest that you submit a ripe piece of fiction or melodramatic epic. But if viewing your personal statement more as creative act than as cold exposition infuses it with personality and reader-friendliness, then give it a try. For example, use some personal possession (e.g., your surfboard) or activity (e.g., equestrianism) that reflects one of your passions as a metaphor for talking about your whole life, connecting specific aspects of that possession or activity to examples from your life that illustrate them. The possibilities for creativity are unlimited.

REVISING AND EDITING

Now that your first draft is done, you must schizophrenically repress the uninhibited Mr. Hyde who created it and summon your editorial Dr. Jekyll to make it presentable. Writing and revising are distinctly different, even opposed, acts. Intermingling them, like trying simultaneously to be a stage actor and theater critic, is to risk misadventure.

Once you've banished your inspired self, your first act as editor is to completely ignore your draft, at least for a day. When you come back to it, you will immediately see things your creative self missed. Before leaping to fix them, step back and consider only macro and organizational changes first, such as contradictory themes or assertions, needlessly repeated points, yawning gaps in context or logic, or weakly developed or poorly placed paragraphs. If you find these, you may need to switch around paragraphs, expunge digressions, or add to, delete, or bolster your examples. By attending to these big-ticket problems first, you'll avoid spit-polishing prose that you later decide to cut.

Depending on how thorough your outline is and how effectively you elaborated on it in your first draft, your personal statement may go through one, two, or even more macro-level revisions before it's ready for editing proper. It's no fun, but you must revise your essays as many times as they require. Continually ask yourself whether your main thesis and secondary points will be clear to the admissions officers, whether your evidence will persuade them, whether you are telling this story as efficiently and clearly as you can. Always choose the simplest, shortest, and most direct expression over the more complex or "sophisticated." Read your essays aloud. Do they flow? Did you notice miscues you missed earlier? Is the tone conversational, and does it sound like you?

Don't try to go through the revision and editing process alone. Whether you ask law advisors, professors, lawyers, or mentors; friends and family; or experienced admissions consultants like those at Accepted.com, seek a reasonable and diverse range of opinions on your personal statement. But take each of them with a grain of salt. Too much positioning and "helpful" tweaking will drain all the personality from your work. They're ultimately your essays; keep it that way.

Revising is really the writing you do after your first draft is done. Editing, on the other hand, is not really composition at all. It is cleaning up the essay's mechanics and grammar at the sentence and word level after the writing is completed. Good lawyers should be good writers, and because they must be adept at precisely the kind of meticulous detail-sifting that effective editing requires, good lawyers should also be good editors.

The changes you make in the editing stage will affect your personal statement less fundamentally, but they will be much more numerous and, if uncorrected, enough in themselves to torpedo an otherwise tightly organized piece of writing. The potential glitches that editing catches can involve everything from pronoun and subject-verb agreement, dangling modifiers, run-on sentences, and parallelism to punctuation and capitalization errors, word choice and misspelling, and active- versus passive-voice issues. If you're uncertain about any of these potential problem areas, review *The Random House Handbook* by Frederick Crews or the redoubtable (and compact) *Elements of Style* by William Strunk, Jr., and E. B. White. Finally, have a trained editor vet your essays.

LETTING GO

Too many applicants decide that their personal statement is "finished" only because the pressure to submit their application early tells them they must be, not because the statement is truly polished. Adcoms are all too used to receiving "revised" essays in the mail from applicants who discovered to their horror errors in already submitted applications. Don't let this happen to you.

Applicants who give themselves enough time risk the opposite danger: obsessively tweaking their essays until they have the bland plasticity of a corporate press release. The personal statement is truly finished when you can't imagine how to make it say what you mean more candidly, vividly, or directly. When you've achieved that level of honesty, color, and tautness—let go.

C H A P T E R

Getting Personal:
The Personal Statement

Imagine a class in which your professor assigns an important paper with the instructions: "Forget formal, academic language—just write naturally, from the heart—and don't do any formal research. I won't grade you on your knowledge of anything outside your own life and interests. Oh, and the specific topic of your paper is your choice—write whatever you want." To most students, that would sound too good to be true, yet it's basically the same instructions that inspire dread in law school applicants writing the personal statement. The very freedom and open-endedness of law schools' essay instructions become a source of anxiety. Rather than respond personally and creatively to schools' open invitations, applicants sniff around for the schools' "real intent" before submitting their best (usually lousy) guess at what the adcoms "want to hear."

Though such anxious second-guessing is understandable, judging by the quality of most application essays, it's ultimately self-defeating. The solution is this: approach the personal statement the way you would our hypothetical professor's assignment—with creative relish. Doing so will not only eliminate some of the stress of the application process, it will give you a much better personal statement.

No matter how you approach it, though, the personal statement will require a great investment of your time and energy. But look on the bright side. You will be able to use it without major changes for almost all your schools, and many schools only require you to write this one essay. Best of all is the personal statement's wide-open scope. You can write about whatever you choose, but if you're stumped for ideas, most schools suggest a range of topics to help you fill up that empty page. Responding effectively to those topics is the subject of this chapter.

WHAT SCHOOLS ASK

"Each candidate must complete, on a separate sheet of paper, a statement presenting any data that may assist the Admissions Committee in rendering a decision." These are typically vague law school essay instructions, right? Actually, these completely unspecific instructions are the exception to the rule. Law schools today rarely give you true carte blanche when it comes to choosing your personal statement's topic. Instead, they nudge you with guidelines that can range from the pinpoint specific—"A brief essay telling why the applicant wishes to obtain a legal education"—to the exhaustive: "The personal statement should tell your 'story' . . . which may include: educational, work or travel experiences, economic disadvantages, significance of extracurricular activities, talents and special interests, involvement in community affairs or public service, colleges attended, course of study, grade trends, graduate work, race or cultural background, and any personal experiences that have influenced your life."

The variety of suggested topics between these two poles is surprisingly broad. Some schools, like Emory, make it abundantly clear that they're using your personal statement to evaluate your writing skills:

> *Personal statement.* Lawyers are professional writers. In our experience, virtually all employers are looking for graduates with superior legal writing skills. Emory devotes substantial education resources to teaching legal writing. . . . Students who come to law school with solid writing skills are in the best position to take advantage of this training. Accordingly, in making admission decisions, Emory looks carefully at writing ability . . .

Got the point yet? Other schools signal that "overcoming obstacles" is a topic they particularly favor:

> Please submit a Personal Statement . . . in which you may bring to the attention of the Admissions Committee anything about yourself that you believe to be relevant to the admission decision. The Admissions Committee will consider the surmounting of economic, social, physical, educational, or other obstacles as evidence bearing on your ability to achieve. If you wish such achievements to be considered, you are encouraged to elaborate upon them in your statement. [Cardozo]

A relatively large number of schools use their personal statement instructions to announce that diversity is their admissions mantra:

> The College of Law is particularly interested in students who, by virtue of their background and experience, will add to the intellectual climate and diversity of the student body. We therefore require that you include a personal statement describing any specific characteristics, background, or experience that would help us achieve our goal of a dynamic and diverse student body. [University of Arizona]

Similarly, schools with religious traditions like Notre Dame may suggest that you show how you share their concerns by asking, "What are your core values?"

And then there are the schools like North Carolina, Loyola Chicago, and Willamette that don't just suggest the topics you may write about, they mandate them. North Carolina, for example, allows you to write about two of six topics, ranging from GPA- or LSAT-related extenuating circumstances, your selection of North Carolina, and unique contribution to their program, to essays about "extreme hardship," "rewarding or disappointing experience," or your preparation for a law career. As we'll see, however, these are the very same topics most schools hope you'll discuss—and that we'll discuss in detail in this chapter.

The majority of law schools, then, throw the door wide open, providing you with an all-inclusive list of topics, but leaving it to you to sort out the ones you like best. You should not respond to these suggested topics by trying to answer each of them, no matter how tempting this may be. You might think you'll earn brownie points by tackling everything, but you'd be mistaken. Even schools that permit up to four-page statements do not give you the room to do justice to the usual gamut of topics in one essay. They offer such a wide range not to elicit a book-length manuscript but to offer you more choices than the usual tired "I've always wanted to be a lawyer" essays. They also realize that not every applicant will have an "obstacle overcome" story or a tale of social disadvantage.

Examine the application forms of the top 70 law schools and you'll see that the topics they suggest can usually be categorized into three general areas:

- *Diversity and obstacles overcome.* How can you add to your class's variety, and can you prove that you deserve a place in it?

- *Accomplishments, strengths, and interests.* Do you have the abilities and track record to convince us you can succeed in law school?

- *Goals.* Have you thought about why you want a law degree and career?

No matter what specific topics or stories you ultimately build your personal statement on, keep these three super-themes at the front of your mind:

1. Uniqueness

2. Ability

3. Motivation

Even if you decide to focus your personal statement on a single life-altering experience, your essay should address all three of these themes, directly or indirectly.

You may be thinking, "It's great that schools help me decide what to write about by listing so many possible topics, but how do I decide which ones are best for me?" Excellent question. The answer is: it will depend on

- Which two or three themes you developed for your self-marketing handle in Chapter 1

- The strengths and emphases of the individual schools you're applying to

- The number of essays each school allows you to write and the topics (assigned or suggested) of those essays

- Your age and career experience (e.g., the "why law?" question must be addressed overtly by older applicants)

- Which of your stories your recommenders will be telling for you

In the end, you should choose the topic (whether suggested by the school or not) that enables you to tell your strongest and most interesting stories, the stories that make you stand out the most and show that you have the proven ability to succeed in law. This is where the inventory you performed in Chapter 1 is key. Your self-marketing handle and data-mining process will have told you what your application's guiding theme is, as well as which stories best illustrate it. So, don't let the schools' suggested topics dictate what you write about or persuade you that you need to write about them all. Instead, be strategically selective. Tell the handful of stories that will portray your qualifications in the strongest and most distinctive light, *whatever* those stories may be—personal, community, academic, professional, or some seamless combination of all four.

For schools like Michigan, which assign you the standard open-ended personal statement as well as your choice of optional essay topics, you will want to put your strongest and most distinctive material in the personal statement and fit your less impressive or less distinctive (though still strong) material into the most appropriate optional essay topic. We discuss how to balance your personal statement against secondary essays in the next chapter.

Few applicants will have a story strong enough to focus their entire essay around. The ones who do (it's often a dramatic "turning point" story) will know it instinctively and shouldn't let themselves be persuaded to dilute it with less powerful material. If you've got it, use it.

Most applicants will decide that their best case can be made with several stories. Their challenge will be to create a unified essay by showing the reader how these stories link together. The easiest, most common, and most effective method is usually the chronological approach: presenting your stories in the order in which they occurred in your life. This does not mean that you write a blow-by-blow autobiography, or that your whole essay must unfold in chronological sequence. To pull the reader in, for example, you might start your essay with a dramatic recent event, then flash back in your second paragraph to an earlier story and begin proceeding forward in time until you return to the opening story at the essay's conclusion. This is exactly what the writer in sample 10 does by opening the essay with the arresting image of an evil dentist run amuck.

You may think the chronological approach is too old school, however, or you may know that your personal statement won't be built around events or experiences. If the focus of your personal statement will be illustrating the key skills or strengths you'll be bringing to law school, for example, you could unify your essay by finding the theme that all these skills or strengths share. Perhaps they are also the skills or strengths that your lawyer mentor possesses. The writer in sample 13, for example, finds an effective unifying device by showing how the strengths she discusses are epitomized by her Grandmother Emma. You could even get more creative and find some activity or object to serve as an overriding metaphor that ties disparate material together. For example, a writer might pull four or five individual stories together by using them to illustrate how fly-fishing is a useful metaphor for the law.

Lest you think that all this talk of strategically selecting your best material means you simply must have awesome stories, remember that *how* you tell your stories can be more important than the material itself. This is the salvation of qualified applicants who really don't have distinct material. By crafting a sincere, personable, interesting essay, they win the adcom over. The quality of your writing—its vividness, its style, its ability to transparently communicate your personality—can force the adcom to shift his or her gaze from the ordinariness of your stories to your engaging self and the compelling way in which you frame or interpret your unremarkable material. Note how the writer of sample 2 infuses his material (none of it devastatingly impressive) with an optimistic, breezily confident tone that enhances his appeal as a candidate.

WHO ARE YOU?: DIVERSITY AND OBSTACLES OVERCOME TOPICS

At the most basic level, the purpose of the personal statement is to show adcoms the person you are behind your numbers. In the absence of interviews and any personal knowledge of you, schools want to get a sense of what you will be like when you're sharing with peers in study group, handling the give and take of your con law class, collaborating with law review colleagues, or representing the school as an alum. On a more practical level, schools are trying to (1) meet their institutional missions to craft varied classes and (2) offer equal educational opportunity to all by recruiting a broad mix of students. These two concerns lie at the heart of the set of topics we discuss in this section.

Law schools signal their interest in the biographical details of your life by embedding language like "background," "influences," and "experiences that have affected your life" in their personal statement instructions. But schools don't want mere autobiography. They're interested in your formative experiences for two reasons: their role in giving you a distinctive perspective on life and the challenges or disadvantages (social, economic, etc.) they show you overcoming. What schools really want is proof that you will bring something unusual and interesting to your class ("diversity") and evidence that you are deserving of admission because of the challenges you've successfully surmounted ("obstacles overcome"). You can give them this, not by trying to shoehorn your entire existence into the essay ("I was born in . . ."), but by narrating a handful of detailed stories that communicate key life experiences. Let's examine the diversity and personal challenge topics one by one.

Diversity

When it comes to shaping law school classes, adcoms' marching orders are "Variety is the spice of life." In terms of occupations alone, typical "T-14" (top-fourteen) law programs have boasted everything from filmmakers and Olympic athletes to ventriloquists and harpsichordists. And the variety only deepens when geographic origins, cultural backgrounds, and personal pursuits are tossed in the pot.

Such rich diversity is the consciously crafted product of schools' judgment that we learn more from those we differ from than from pale reflections of ourselves. Because the word *diversity* still carries an affirmative action tinge, however, many applicants assume they're out of luck in the diversity department unless their grandmother was Mohican. Though it's true that schools show special favor to applicants from U.S. underrepresented minority groups—primarily, African Americans, Hispanic Americans, and Native Americans—admissions statistics prove that law schools define *diversity* much more widely than in strictly ethnic terms.

By suggesting diversity topics for your personal statement, admissions committees are inviting you to help them sculpt that class of maximum variety. The pressure is on you to "demonstrate" your diversity, to convince the schools that you can enhance your classmates' experience more profoundly than the next applicant. How you accomplish that demonstration is left mostly up to you. "What do *you* think makes you unique?" the diversity question asks; "What do *you* think your distinct contribution to your class will be?"

One way of knowing which aspects of your profile are really "diverse" is by simply inventorying your life, as discussed in Chapter 1. Start with the narrow, conventional definitions of diversity—race, ethnic background, or disability. If you are an underrepresented minority or a disabled applicant, then consider discussing that fact to whatever depth will capture its importance in your life. Note how effectively the writer of sample 21 uses his story of permanent nerve damage to demonstrate his ability to succeed creatively. Next, look at socioeconomic, cultural, and geographic types of diversity. If you overcame an economically disadvantaged childhood, identify strongly with your family's cultural roots, or come from a foreign country or a U.S. region underrepresented at your target school, these are diversity factors on which you will want to expand in your personal statement.

Consider also your community activities and hobbies. If they play central roles in your life or are atypical, they may also deserve a prominent place in your essay. In fact, schools like University of Oregon *require* you to write about "significant community activities." Your education may have been unusual (e.g., your school's location or affiliation, your major or scholarships). Your specific profession and industry choice can also enhance your diversity; your religious or spiritual life may be significant and unusual; and your post-JD goals may set you apart. Even your age, sexuality, or specific family dynamics (if handled properly) may convince law schools that your contribution could be distinctive. Skills or areas of expertise, unusual or challenging life experiences, even personal qualities or traits such as the gift of humor are all valid, potentially fruitful diversity topics.

If, after drawing up your personal diversity inventory, you still think you're too "unexceptional," don't fret. A diverse class doesn't mean a class filled with demographic outliers; it also means one that includes a goodly number of strong applicants with traditional, "middle-of-the-road" profiles. If you feel that's you, then tell your "normality" tale as engagingly and vividly as you can. Your charm and winning presentation can themselves create the sense of potential contribution that schools look for. Personality, in other words, can be a "diversity factor." Your diversity elements may not be terribly unusual taken individually, but together they may well make you memorably distinct. The modest humor employed by the writer of sample 5 goes a long way toward establishing him as the kind of appealing personality law schools would like to have around.

Aside from the content you choose, what can you do to ensure that your personal statement really convinces admissions officers that you can make a significant and distinctive addition to the class? First, you must provide vivid details and concrete examples; they will automatically individuate you because they're specific to your life. Since the words or themes you will use to label your uniqueness have probably been used before, it's your examples that will give your personal statement its real singularity. Make sure they have color and bite. Second, it's not enough to simply name your diversity factors—"I am an

African American who grew up in Idaho"—and drop in a few examples. You must also explicitly state how your diversity or uniqueness factors have benefited or educated you, what they've added to your life and could add to classmates' lives, and perhaps even how they contributed to your decision to study law. For example, what life lessons or insights did you gain from growing up in Mozambique, or abandoning your budding career as a rock musician, or chasing your passion for Tang Dynasty antiques to Nepal? And in what ways will you share these lessons or insights with your future classmates? If you can, show schools that you've already begun envisioning how to share your special traits and interests within their programs.

Another key way to address law schools' diversity topics is to highlight your international or cross-cultural experiences. Law schools value international exposure, not only because new perspectives deepen the classroom learning experience, but because global experiences often go hand in hand with personal growth, tolerance, and enhanced professional value. Beware: international experiences do not mean tourist travel experiences. Adcoms read many insipid travelogues about swaying palm trees in Cancun or speaking Français with real Parisians. They rarely find them interesting or edifying. Samples 3 and 8 work in part because the international experiences they recount (in Kuwait and Guyana, respectively) are not only distinctive but sustained and formative.

Even applicants who were not raised in Borneo or schooled in Vladivostok can write vivid and compelling international stories that show depth of insight and reflection on how their cross-cultural experience affected them. Ask yourself, "What did my international experience teach me about people, my country, human difference (or basic sameness), or myself?" The author of sample 23, for example, cannot finally claim to be much more than a child of immigrants, but by weaving together the importance of his Polish heritage, brief stays in Spain and Israel, and his multilingual skills he presents a compellingly international self-portrait.

Obstacles Overcome

The other main reason law schools suggest you write about your personal "background" is to learn about challenges you may have overcome. They want to know whether there are legitimate reasons to overlook less-than-competitive numbers and reward applicants who have succeeded despite, as Boalt Hall bluntly puts it, "various types of hardship, each of which tend to correlate highly with some racial and ethnic backgrounds." They also want evidence that you can surmount major challenges because surviving law school will be a significant test of your will and focus.

Not all personal challenges will have the same value, of course. Schools will be especially sensitive to stories by applicants "not ordinarily well represented in the student body" (as one school puts it) about overcoming extreme poverty, unusually painful setbacks or personal losses, a physical handicap, or prejudice or other social hardships. They will have considerably less interest in "obstacle" stories about struggling to come to terms with one's affluent upbringing, losing 20 pounds to make varsity, or overcoming the emotional devastation of a deceased pet. If you're uncertain whether your story will be seen as a true challenge or disadvantage, then listen to your doubts and choose another story—it probably isn't strong enough—or get feedback from others.

You do not need to and should not feel compelled to include an obstacle-overcome story in your personal statement if you don't have a strong one. You can still persuade the admissions committee that you are a deserving and distinctive candidate with real determination by focusing your personal statement on a sincere, self-knowing, and well-executed dramatization of a single challenging, defining, or revealing moment in your life.

Half the battle is identifying that event. It does not need to be some traumatic, movie-of-the-week moment (though those don't hurt), but it does have to have left you a different person. A defining moment can mean an inflection or turning point when you had to change your thinking or outlook fundamentally. Sample 3 is an example of a turning-point essay nested inside a career-progress essay. The writer, dissatisfied with his engineering career, becomes intrigued by the kinds of questions the law raises while taking a professional seminar. It takes the tragic death of a friend to transform these academic lessons about the law into a career-changing wake-up call.

When applicants have truly powerful events to narrate, there is sometimes a tendency to overplay one's hand, either by writing about the event in over-wrought prose or by focusing too much on the event rather than on one's reaction to it. Resist these urges. Let the events communicate their own power through the vividness of your description and make sure that you remain the subject of the essay.

One form of the defining-moment or significant-event essay is the "encounter with the law," often a crime observed or some other personal exposure to the law in action. Sample 18 is one compelling example. To avoid suspicions of shallowness, you may want to avoid defining moments from your work life, though even these will work if they had unusual and far-reaching impact on you personally and professionally (see the discussion of accomplishments later in this chapter). You should also resist the temptation to discuss romantic relationships. However defining they may have been, they often aren't unusual or relevant enough to merit an essay.

Don't let your description of the event itself crowd out the takeaways. You need a section that describes your feelings about the event and how it changed you emotionally or "inwardly."

Don't expect the power of the moment to speak for itself, even if it's traumatic enough to seem obvious. Admissions committees want you to walk them through the lessons and subsequent life changes. And whether the defining moment itself was positive or not, you want the lessons learned to be uplifting—at least to the extent that they made you a better, wiser person. As much as possible, let the reader inside. Candidly describe your emotions in response to the event and your thought processes while coming to grips with and moving on from it. But describe them calmly and maturely. You want the schools to admire you, not pity you.

You also need a section detailing how you have translated the internal change caused by the defining moment into action. Unless your defining moment is of the "encounter with the law" type, you should resist the temptation to say that its impact was the realization that you really need a law degree. Admissions officers hear that all the time and, usually, don't believe a word of it.

ACCOMPLISHMENTS, STRENGTHS, AND INTERESTS

Whereas the diversity and personal background topics seek to know who you are, this second group of topics seeks to know what you've done (accomplishments) or what you're good at (strengths, abilities, interests). By suggesting that you write about such topics as "achievements," "qualifications," "evidence of . . . leadership and responsibility," or "significant or extracurricular activities, talents, and special interests," law schools are signaling that they want tangible evidence that you can perform the hard work of legal study and know how to translate your values and dreams into results.

Accomplishments

Are your accomplishments substantial enough to show that you can handle the Sturm und Drang of law school? Which of your achievements—academic, professional, community, or personal—show that you actually have the potential to become a lawyer? How have you translated your skills or passions into concrete results that demonstrably prove your "qualifications" for law school? The magnitude of the achievements you choose to describe helps to answer these key questions. And the details you convey about your accomplishments will prove your ability to analyze complex problems, cope with the brutal realities and uncertainties of law school, and eventually contribute to the legal profession.

Former admissions officer James Strachan usefully defines an accomplishment as "an event or situation in which you successfully exerted a high degree of influence resulting in a sense of personal satisfaction that allowed you to learn something about yourself." That's a pretty broad definition, but it accurately reflects the scope that law schools are willing to give you. In choosing which of your stories to wrap around this definition, start by asking yourself three questions:

1. What am I—off the record and in all candor—truly proudest of?

2. When have I had the greatest tangible impact on an institution, organization, or others?

3. When has a positive experience in which I played a key role *changed* me or *taught* me the most?

Defining *accomplishment* as loosely as possible, sift through your memory, scrutinize your résumé, and interrogate your friends or colleagues. Chances are you'll find a story in which the depth of your impact was substantial and concretely, externally visible; one whose lessons you're still applying today and look back on with a quiet sense of pride. If you do, you have the makings of a killer accomplishment essay. If this brainstorm exercise generates too many candidates, revisit the self-marketing themes you created in Chapter 1. Which of your accomplishments best supports your application's themes or influenced your decision to attend law school?

The accomplishment you choose to write about tells adcoms what experiences you value most in your life. The applicant who writes about a debate contest she won in high school sends a very different message from the candidate whose crowning moment was chairing his community organization's fund drive. Because law schools give you so much freedom, you need to evaluate the accomplishment stories you choose with extra caution. Think carefully before saying that your accomplishment was getting into an Ivy League college or scoring the winning touchdown in your high school championship game. Unless you execute these well-worn topics extremely well (and even when you do), you may give the impression that you have a narrowly competitive or superficial definition of achievement or that you're living in the past, with no significant accomplishments since the onset of adulthood.

Exactly which of your stories has the potential to make admissions officers sit up and actually feel enthusiasm is sometimes hard for you to gauge on your own. Talking through your options with friends, your prelaw advisor, or an admissions consultant may help you view your material more objectively. Naturally, the applicant who can say that her achievement led directly to an award-winning thesis or a multimillion-dollar revenue gain has an advantage over the applicant whose "greatest achievement" was earning an A in Ancient Urdu or helping teammates in an aborted project with no bottom-line impact.

If you're applying with several years of work experience, you should not focus your personal statement on an academic achievement. Law schools and the firms that recruit their graduates are increasingly favoring students who enter law school with at least a few years of full-time work experience. If you have that professional exposure, schools will be interested in hearing what you've done with it and how it has shaped your professional plans. Since working as a paralegal is a profile law adcoms see all too often, the shrewd applicant will have devoted his or her post-college years to a career that brought greater responsibility and broader skills then paralegals typically acquire. Whether that position is related to the law indirectly (such as working for a congressman, government agency, or NGO) or not at all is immaterial to admissions committees. But paralegal work after college may actually harm your chances.

Applicants applying from college or soon after graduation should consider making their extracurricular or community involvements the subject of an accomplishment-focused personal statement. Your extracurricular activities tell adcoms what values express themselves in your free-time pursuits and also how effectively you will function in the formal and informal group activities that define the law school experience. And since many law school applicants are too young to have gained significant leadership experience at work, adcoms also look to these extracurricular-focused essays for evidence of your leadership potential. If your nonwork commitments involve helping your community, especially in a leadership role, you'll be demonstrating the selflessness that admissions officers like to see in students and alumni. Finally, the history of your involvements tells schools how deeply you can commit to and focus on the things you care about.

Many applicants seem to assume their accomplishments are being graded in bulk terms: the more activities they mention, the more impressed law schools will be. The truth is that essays focusing on your lifelong interest in one or two activities (no matter how many other activities you're also passionate about) will almost always go over better. Rather than provide an exhaustive survey of your nonwork pursuits, then, steer the essay toward the activities that matter most to you, consume most of your free time, and ideally demonstrate skills related to law school (such as writing, research, leadership, or public interest work). If your best extracurricular achievements are your annual Christmas trips with your family to help at a local soup kitchen, focus your personal statement on another topic.

Applicants fortunate enough to have truly standout accomplishments—becoming a congressman's chief aide at 25, producing your own award-winning indie film, earning a Fulbright Scholarship, taking the helm of a nuclear submarine, leading a $40 million IPO at 26, earning a spot on an Olympic team—should build their personal statements around them. In studying under Senator Bill Bradley, encountering Washington's elite on *Meet the Press*, and seeing a national political convention from the inside, the author of sample 22 has a wealth of standout accomplishments to talk about—and he finds a way to make them all part of his story.

Fortunately for less-accomplished applicants, law schools are interested in *you* much more than the "objective" magnitude of your achievement. Effective accomplishment essays combine distinctiveness in the actual attainment itself with a special zest, depth, or personality in the telling and analysis. *How* you describe your accomplishments tells the admissions committee a great deal. If your accomplishments are impressive, but you create the impression that you rammed them through with no regard for others, law schools may question your interpersonal skills and integrity. Similarly, the committee will also pay close attention to the reasons you give for valuing this accomplishment. If you say only that you're proud of this achievement because it earned you a magna cum laude or led to an early promotion, they'll wonder why it didn't teach you deeper lessons.

The strengths that your achievement illustrates should corroborate the strengths you emphasize across your application. If your post-JD goals, recommendation letters, and other essays market you as an unusually global applicant, you will want your personal statement to highlight an attainment with an international dimension. Ideally, you also want your accomplishments to show that you made an impact in multiple ways. A professional success, for example, might show you deploying both analytical skill and team leadership. Similarly, a community achievement could show you succeeding through teamwork and consensus building, and a personal triumph through, say, creativity and risk-taking.

Also be sure to calibrate the accomplishment you choose against the school's self-image. A personal statement that subtly communicates that you've devoted every waking moment to feathering your own nest may be poorly received at a school that prides itself on producing public-interest lawyers or government employees.

An accomplishment-focused personal statement, then, is considerably more than a résumé bullet point writ large. In fact, the "what" of your achievement is only one of four components that most effective accomplishment essays have in common:

1. Context and challenge

2. The achievement itself

3. The outcome

4. The accomplishment's significance to you

The first paragraph or so of a good accomplishment-focused personal statement draws the reader into the essay in an engaging, vivid way. It "sets the scene" by providing a rough time frame for the action and just enough context so the reader understands the enormity of the challenge you faced. The writer of sample 25 instantly magnifies the significance of his achievement by devoting one sentence to all the hurdles that stood in his way: "My handicaps in this experiment were a relatively small ownership position, secondary status as an out-of-towner, and a board that unanimously (at least publicly) refused to admit it had underperformed and adamantly opposed any change that might threaten its local stature."

Many applicants devote prodigious swaths of their essays to meticulous accounts of their achievement: "I did X . . ., then I did Y . . ." The true payoff of the accomplishment essay comes at its end, however. So it is essential that you minimize your treatment of the achievement to the key events, with special emphasis on the variety of ways in which you tackled the challenge.

Since an accomplishment essay is a story, if you can give it the drama of a good tale, you may lift it above the crowd. The use of plot "twists" or "complications," unexpected detours, and moments of self-doubt or uncertainty add texture and interest, transforming the tedious exposition of a career data point into the kind of human-interest story admissions officers may remember. So, if you experienced some initial missteps before you experienced success, don't be afraid to describe them. They'll give your accomplishment true grit by showing you have the maturity to "own up" to errors and overcome multiple challenges. Note, for example, how the applicant in sample 17 gives her "passion for social justice" credibility by describing her frustrated disappointment when one of her homeless clients fails to give her the happy ending she has worked so hard for.

A clear statement of the ultimate outcome of your achievement gives your story closure and provides the hard evidence to back up your claim of success. Although law schools value the subjective lessons you draw from your accomplishments as well as their "objective" bottom-line impact, not just any subjective evaluation will do. The specific significance you place on your accomplishment tells schools how thoughtful or self-reflective you are, what you value (e.g., personal benefits versus social benefits), and how deeply you learn from new experiences.

Fortunately for many applicants, the emphasis schools place on your subjective evaluation of your accomplishment gives you the opportunity to turn unimpressive bottom-line achievements into fabulous tales of personal growth and inner challenge. As Michigan notes, "The personal statement should not be a mere catalog of accomplishments and activities but a thoughtful explanation of what those accomplishments and activities have meant to you." A deeply insightful analysis of your achievement's value may pull you "equal" to a star achiever who merely phones in the takeaways. Your accomplishment's significance and the life lessons it has taught you must be genuine and personal to you. Unfortunately, the only way to make them so is to be honestly introspective and really explore the experience's impact on you. Then describe that as directly and un-self-consciously as you can.

Avoid any lesson learned that smacks of superficiality: "It was my most significant achievement because it led directly to my promotion four months later." The significance statement should aim for deeper payoffs than just raises and promotions (though you can refer to these as the evidence or outcome of your accomplishment). Also avoid asserting lessons that sound like the kind of thing you think schools want to hear: "This experience was profoundly valuable to me because it offered me the humbling privilege of giving back to the less fortunate in my community in a meaningful way." This reeks of insincerity, whether the writer meant it or not. In contrast, note how the writer of sample 4 anchors her description of an extraordinary accomplishment—winning the Women's World Sailing Championships—with a meaty paragraph on the lessons of teamwork and pacing that made that success possible.

Strengths and Interests

Focusing your personal statement on strength-related topics—"personal traits," "distinctive qualities and talents," "special interests"—is another way to show law schools that you are not only deserving of admission, but qualified for it. Do you have a mature, balanced understanding of yourself? Do you have the personal traits that law schools search for, namely the ability to synthesize knowledge, a tolerance for ambiguity, the capacity to see all sides of an issue, a sense of justice, drive and determination, intellectual and personal well-roundedness? More practically, can you show that you have the writing, analysis, and interpersonal skills lawyers need? And have you demonstrated any of these strengths or skills through your personal passions? By using your personal statement to answer these questions you can turn it into a proactive case for your own admission.

The strengths you discuss in this essay must complement (if not entirely overlap) the strengths your recommenders cite and those that your application as a whole communicates. Naturally, all law schools value persistence, intelligence, and writing and analytical skills, but your personal statement should blend these "obligatory" strengths with characteristics that are really personal to you, like leadership or creativity. Closely examine schools' personal statement instructions, and you'll find that many tend to favor language-related skills (such as knowledge of foreign languages) and intellectual abilities (as evidenced by advanced studies, etc.). Harvard is typical of many such schools in its suggestion that you write about "a course, academic project, book, artistic or cultural experience that has been important to you."

The laziest and most common structure for strength essays is to take up each quality in turn, illustrate it with an example, and then awkwardly transition on to the next: "My second greatest strength is my . . ." To avoid this antidote for insomnia, find some common element or quality that your strengths share and weave your essay around that, or, better yet, find a single story (a work project, for example) or activity (e.g., bungee jumping) that will illustrate all your strengths and weaknesses in one fell swoop. It's awfully hard to be original when discussing traits you probably share with most of humanity, so remember that in strength-focused personal statements you can make yourself stand out by projecting a distinctive combination of strengths illustrated by stories unique to your life.

Strength or qualification essays are ideal for applicants who don't have a powerful defining moment, accomplishment, or diversity story to tell or who have several stories whose interconnection is not immediately obvious. The writer in sample 2, for example, manages to skillfully integrate his trip to Masada in Israel, his love of music, and his community involvements by showing how each illustrates his ability to bring people together. Likewise, the writer in sample 4 uses the overriding metaphor of sailing to link her journey toward a law career. In sample 7, the writer's special ability to find creative solutions serves as an umbrella theme for linking stories about varsity debate, music, advising students, and teaching. And in sample 19, the applicant uses the skills of risk-taking to unify a staggering variety of impressive but not obviously related accomplishments.

Focusing your personal statement on a "special interest" or hobby can allow you to combine evidence of what you're capable of achieving when you follow your passions with personal insights that may help you stand out from the crowd—and thus make you a "diversity" admission candidate. How you spend your free time can say more about you then what you do in the classroom or workplace where your choices are often decided by someone else. Whether you enjoy volunteering as a dance instructor, collecting antiques, weight training, or working as a math tutor, demonstrating an enthusiast's knowledge of an obscure subject and/or dramatizing your passion through a specific memorable experience can produce a personal statement of grit and distinctiveness. Consider focusing on the hobbies that may offset the negative stereotypes every profile drags behind it. If you're a computer programmer, for example, writing about your love of math puzzles may reinforce adcoms' leadership concerns, but an essay about your leadership of a deep-sea archaeology team will surprise them in the best possible way.

As always, it's not enough simply to describe your interest. You must account for your enjoyment of it, perhaps by explaining how you first became involved in it or by describing your emotional state while you're pursuing it. Has your long pursuit of this passion changed you or taught you anything about yourself or life? Better yet, if pursuing your passion has somehow enabled you to benefit others, say so and provide any hard evidence that substantiates this. You must make the reader experience your genuine enthusiasm for your personal involvements, and you must make him or her understand why.

Some experts will caution you to avoid focusing on passions that are controversial, such as politics or religion. But if your views are not too doctrinaire or far from the mainstream and you focus on the positive results they've inspired you to achieve, then you shouldn't feel you have to kill a good essay for fear of offending someone. Adcoms are professional enough to restrain their biases long enough to appreciate your passion and achievements.

Personal statements that focus on "special interests" can sometimes take the form of abstract, long-winded analyses of issues meaningful to you—the dreaded "think piece." Be forewarned that these usually fall flat because they don't focus on you, and the quality of your analysis may not be as compelling as you imagine. (Remember, law professors will be among your readers!) But if the issue is integral to your passion for a cause and you keep the focus on the connection between the cause and your own life, give it a whirl—but show it to others to see if it works. Adcoms want to know about you, not the history of anti-clear-cutting law in Oregon's logging industry.

GOALS

The vast majority of law schools include goals among their suggested personal statement topics because—surprise—they want to know what reasons motivate you to go to all the trouble, expense, and opportunity cost of earning a JD. Do you really have more than a vague or passing interest in the law as a practical profession? Schools know all too well that many applicants seek law degrees for the "wrong" reasons—not because the JD really prepares them for a career they've attained some understanding of and want to commit their adult lives to. Goal-related personal statements give law schools a way to police the realism of their applicants' aspirations.

A second reason is that admissions officers, like everyone else, respond to enthusiasm. Projecting a knowledgeable and well-defined reason for law school—and theirs in particular—conveys credible, personal enthusiasm. "I need a JD to use my skills to become the best attorney I can be" won't generate much excitement, but a detailed, astute paragraph in place of this sentence could. Especially for older applicants who've been in the work world for a few years, the personal statement gives adcoms a chance to do a reality check on maturity and career savvy.

Third, schools also use personal statements to make a read on the quality of your mind and character. Are you a realistic person or a vague or flaky dreamer? Can you craft a compelling case in prose that links your past, present, and future?

Why the Law?

There are dozens of excellent reasons for choosing a law career. Unfortunately, they tend not to be the reasons that many applicants cite! If you recognize yourself in any of the following, don't begin writing your personal statement until you've come up with something better:

- ■ "I have the numbers [LSAT, GPA] to get into a good law school."

- ■ "My friends or peers are in law school," or "My parents are lawyers and expect me to be too."

- ■ "Post-JD starting salaries are high."

- ■ "I majored in history [English, philosophy, political science] and it's either law school or drive a cab."

- ■ "Because I'm a big fan of [insert name of latest TV show or novel with law theme]."

- ■ "I think I'd be good at it," "I love to argue," or "Everyone says I'd be a great lawyer."

- ■ "I was just downsized and have nothing else to do."

- ■ "I have a master's and another degree will look really impressive."

- ■ "I'm fascinated by law as an intellectual construct and can't wait to study its history and manifestations in different societies."

Though these are common reasons for applying to law school, they all share the same drawback: they won't impress admissions committees. In all likelihood, it's some combination of intellectual challenge, income potential, and interest in a career that benefits others that draws you. But if you do decide to explore the "why the law?" topic in your personal statement, these should be only your starting points (and the income motivation should always remain unstated).

Don't assume, however, that a law school personal statement *must* explain why you've decided to become a lawyer. Most undergraduates don't have enough exposure to the law to advance compelling reasons for their decision and so wind up boring or aggravating adcoms when they could be charming or wowing them. "Why I want to go to law school" is the one topic adcoms see most often, and they can be forgiven for being weary of it. So, unless your target school is among the few that require you to address this question, it's quite acceptable to take a chance and focus your essay on something else, perhaps broaching the "why the law?" question in your closing paragraph, if at all. If you're still in college or have recently graduated, personal statements built around your personal background, accomplishments, or strengths, as discussed earlier in this chapter, may be the better bet.

If you are an older applicant who's been in the world for a few years though, "why the law?" must occupy a central place in your personal statement. You have no choice but to explain as specifically as possible where your law school goals came from and why you know you will enjoy this field and succeed in it. You can explain this based on the interests you've developed in your current career and the exposure you've gained to the law through your current work, community experience, professional network, or personal research. Explain why you chose your current career, then how you realized it was not ideal for you (the negative explanation) and/or how your exposure to the law showed you it was a better career choice for you (the positive explanation). The writer in sample 11 was inspired to pursue a career in international intellectual property law because of his experiences as a financial analyst/planner, business development manager, and marketing manager with Pacific Rim technology companies. Likewise, the applicant in sample 14 arrived at his legal goals as an IT consultant through interacting with corporate attorneys at Eli Lilly. And the author of sample 20 developed an interest in intellectual property law when colleagues at his IT firm began purchasing domain names based on celebrities' names and worried about the legal ramifications.

Stating that you want to make a career switch does not mean dwelling on your loathing for your current career, of course. You can describe the limitations of your current career track without sounding desperate or trashing your current employer. If your work experience didn't expose you to the law, explain what did. Perhaps a purely personal experience opened your eyes. Describe it. Maybe a dramatic and unexpected encounter with the power or complexity of the law sparked your deep interest. If so, your personal statement may resemble the defining moment topic we discussed earlier. Perhaps a friend's advice or a news article hinted that this particular career path might best match your personality, so you followed up with personal research and informational interviews. The author of sample 24 turned to law school to gain the skills needed to protect the mission of his family's philanthropic foundation. The applicant in sample 25 discovered that law was his calling when the sorry management of a company his family had invested in prompted him to use his shareholder rights to force a litigious solution. And the writer in sample 26 became intrigued by the law while serving as a volunteer interpreter for a Chinese woman with legal problems. Whatever your particular story, let the admissions committee in on the origins of your goals. And demonstrate that you've done your due diligence in learning what a law career is really about.

In tracing how you came to the law, avoid a bland recitation of your résumé in sentence form: "Then I . . . and then I . . . and then . . ." Schools will only be interested in the inflection points, the key career decisions. Dig for such inflection points by interrogating yourself about your biggest career decisions. Why has your career taken the trajectory it has? What have you learned about your abilities and potential as your career has unfolded? Insert mini-accomplishments that illustrate the pivotal moments in your path toward discovering the law as your calling. For maximum effect, try to quantify the impact of these accomplishments and highlight what was atypical or "fast-track" about your path relative to peers. Your evolving career goals, in other words, can be the "takeaways" or lessons you learned from these mini-accomplishments.

By laying this interpretive, evaluative narrative over your career, you can instruct the admissions committees in how to properly view the raw data of your résumé, eliminate their specific questions or concerns about your work experience, and provide them with a context for feeling good about your decision to choose the law. Put another way, a personal statement that explains how you arrived at your decision to study law but fails to mention key career choices or pivotal moments is a wasted opportunity to emphasize your strengths. It invites adcoms to provide their own, perhaps less favorable, explanations for the career choices you've left unexplained. By the same token, a personal statement built around professional accomplishments, no matter how superb, will fail if you can't show how they relate to your need for a law degree.

A riskier and less common strategy for addressing the "why the law?" question is to explain why the law appeals to you as a way of thinking. The risks here are numerous. You may come across as naïvely uninformed about the overwhelmingly technical and practical nature of the law; you may display a lack of knowledge about the law itself (remember those law professor readers!); or you may convince adcoms that you deserve admission, not to a law program, but to a graduate humanities program in the history of comparative legal thought. Still, if this "intellectual" approach accurately captures your motivation for the law and you can talk convincingly about the law in an intelligent, even learned, fashion, then this may work for you, as it did for the author of sample 15. By leveraging his early interest in writing, he demonstrates an appreciation for the interconnection of law and language, which he elaborates by discussing the ambiguities of legal language and the philosophical questions raised by a particular case. (But it doesn't hurt that he concludes the essay by showing that he also has firsthand experience with the nitty-gritty of probate law.)

Avoid at all costs the "I've always wanted to be a lawyer" approach: "When I was six I could cite chapter and verse of *Blackstone's Commentaries* and personally researched and wrote all the summonses I served on unsuspecting neighbors." Applicants who adopt this strategy assume they don't need to know *why* they want to become lawyers so long as they can prove that ambition is ardent and deep-seated. Adcoms aren't buying it.

Getting Specific

As noted, law schools don't expect younger applicants to have sufficient exposure to the law to be able to state what fields within law they expect to practice. But since the law encompasses a variety of specialties and few lawyers are true generalists anymore, if you do have enough of an idea—based on concrete exposure to the law or lawyers—to sketch out some possible paths, consider doing so. Some schools show their interest in this information by specifically asking whether you have an interest in special areas of the law in a separate question on the application form. If you really don't know, don't fake it; adcoms will see through it. If you are an older applicant, you have no choice but to indicate one or two practice areas in which you envision your career unfolding.

Though most applicants probably envision careers as well-remunerated attorneys at mammoth big-city firms, most real lawyers work in much smaller practices and in niches more varied than you might imagine. Certain practice areas tend to become "in" (e.g., intellectual property, trial law), so if you state them as your intended specialty make sure your personal statement shows you have some real sense of what they involve. Indicating an interest in unglamorous, nitty-gritty practice areas like bankruptcy law, probate, arbitration, or appellate law, if fleshed out with believable stories, may help strengthen your "why the law?" story. One benefit of being able to discuss possible specializations is that you can then tailor your personal statement to emphasize your target schools' strengths in these areas (more on this in the next section).

The post-JD career plan most often named in personal statements is undoubtedly public interest law. Many applicants are idealistic about the law or believe that stating altruistic goals will separate them in the adcoms' minds from the mass of applicants merely looking to gild their nests as corporate attorneys. In fact, only between 2 and 5 percent of all JDs actually wind up practicing public interest law. So even if adcoms viewed public interest goals with special favor—and they do not—the fact that so many applicants claim them should convince you not to, unless you've got the stories to make those goals credible. To overcome adcoms' skepticism, you must be able to show through your work or extracurricular experience that public service has been a long-standing motivation for you.

If public interest law is indeed an aspect of your career plan, you need not propose that your post-JD goal is to "save the world." Since law firms are legally required to provide free public services, you might simply indicate the area of pro bono work you hope to focus on as an attorney. That is, you do not have to claim that you plan to work for a Legal Aid clinic to make the case that you are attracted to law for its positive social benefits. Try to craft a more nuanced and credible justification for your idealistic legal ambitions. Stanford Law School's apologia from the 1970s shows it can be done without sounding like Mother Teresa: "Lawyers are among the most active participants in the process of working out accommodations and solutions to human problems; for the first-class lawyer is an unusually productive mix of technician, analyst, gladiator, counselor, tactician, institutional architect, politician and scholar."

Why Our School?

Yes, you probably could submit the same personal statement to all the schools on your target list. But why be lazy when so much is at stake? If you expect your application to stand out, you should customize each essay with language that links your educational needs to the specific offerings and culture of each school.

An effective "why our school?" section must begin with serious personal research on the school, not just a quick skim of the school's Web site and ABA and LSAC's *Official Guide*. While it's true that you won't find much variety in first-year law curricula, law schools are hardly homogeneous. Show each school that you value its unique self-image.

Don't just list the school's attractive features in numbered order. If a school's curricular resources perfectly complement your intended specialization, then you could devote more space to these academic factors. But the best customization strategy is to build on your interactions with people at that school. A visit to the school is strongly advised, unless it's financially impossible. Even attending information sessions in your city can give you a better sense of the school than impersonal research. Consider talking about your campus visit first and giving it the most space. Walk the adcoms through your discovery process: how you learned about the school, with an emphasis on people-oriented research—visits, conversations with alumni attorneys, e-mails to students, and so on.

Avoid wasting space on any selection factor that could also be said of any other school. "Elite Law School is my first choice because it uniquely offers renowned faculty, hands-on clinical programs, multiple law journal opportunities, and a diverse range of electives." Uniquely? Virtually every school accredited by the American Bar Association could claim that this sentence described it. You must refer by name to aspects of the school's program that will individualize your areas of interest. For example, almost all law schools have law journals, but only the University of Kentucky has a *Journal of Mineral Resources and Environmental Law*. Every law school offers a decent variety of electives, but only Boalt Hall and Rutgers offer Modern Chinese Law and Human Sexuality and the Law, respectively. Simply by citing these features by name you lift your "why our school?" section one level above the typical applicant's. And if you tie these distinctive areas of interest to your interests and goals, you'll earn bonus points.

As a rough guide, your "why our school?" section may touch on four categories of school-specific information:

1. *Academics.* This includes everything from academic tracks or specialties, specific courses, and clinical and moot court opportunities to faculty members (including research interest), teacher-to-student ratio, and joint-degree opportunities. *Hint:* Research books, articles, or case studies by professors whose interests match yours. Consider mentioning one or two of these publications in your essay to show the school you've done your homework.

2. *Extracurricular features.* You can refer to everything from law journals, alumni networks, student clubs, and "bar review" nights on the town to externships, overseas or exchange opportunities, and community involvement initiatives. *Hint:* If the school has no organization in one of your interest areas, consider stating that you will start one (if you would). Adcoms may be impressed by your initiative.

3. *General and "cultural" features.* This is where you show that you understand the school's specific culture or self-image, the message it sends about what it believes makes it unique. You might discuss anything from class size and urban-versus-rural location to percentage of minority students, religious affiliation, or faculty association with a particular school of thought (such as the critical legal studies movement). *Hint:* Refer to the notes you took during your school selection process. Many of the reasons you originally used to winnow your list can actually be mentioned in this section, so long as you also link them to specific school resources by name.

4. *Campus visit and personal interaction.* Making a campus visit is an excellent way to show interest. Capitalize on your visit by noting which classes you sat in on, which adcoms and students you spoke with (by name), and what you learned about the school that you didn't know before. You can use all this information in your personal statement or secondary essays to personalize your "why our school?" message. But such personalization can also extend beyond a campus visit. If you know alumni, mention them by name and tell how you know them and what you have learned from them about the school. *Hint:* Consider contacting one or two faculty members whose research interests match yours and arranging to discuss your interests with them. You can then refer to these conversations in your essay.

As the sample personal statements at the back of this book demonstrate, your "why our school?" need not be lengthy to be effective. The applicant in sample 20 not only names specific courses that attract him, but connects them explicitly to his interests and past experience. The candidate in sample 9 leverages her status as an alumna of her target law school's university by referring to a former professor's recommendation that she apply to her alma mater's law program. The applicants in samples 10 and 13 shrewdly make clear that they have ties to their target schools' communities and intend to practice there after their degrees. Sample 22 shows an applicant deploying the ultimate form of personalization: noting that he's applying on the recommendation of a very special alumnus—his father. Finally, in sample 29 answering the "why our school?" question becomes the entire point of the essay, as the writer makes a successful case for transferring to the University of Chicago.

Just as you may decide that addressing your reasons for law school in the personal statement won't strengthen your application, it's also possible you'll conclude that a "why our school?" section weakens your statement's impact or appears "tacked on." That's fine. Don't make your personal statement take on more than it comfortably can. Some schools require you to explain "why us?" in the personal statement, but most do not. And as we'll see in the next chapter, most schools give you opportunities to use the material you left out of the personal statement.

3

Finishing Strong: Secondary Essays and Wait-List Letters

Appearances perhaps to the contrary, law school adcoms are not sadists. The best proof, aside from a personal statement whose focus *you* get to decide, is that you have one more chance, and sometimes more, to make your case for admission—through the secondary essay. For our purposes, the *secondary essay* means all the essays that law schools require or allow you to submit besides the main personal statement. For some law schools, the secondary essay is a mandatory essay on a specific topic, such as the University of Tennessee's requirement that you write a 500-word essay on "one of the most important learning experiences you have had in the past 10 years." But for most schools the secondary essay comes in one of two flavors—the optional essay and the addendum. What's the difference? The optional essay is longer, may focus on a specific topic or let you to choose your own, and will only be considered optional by the unsavvy applicant. The addendum, in contrast, should be a short statement, not a full-dress essay, that focuses on a narrow range of extenuating circumstances and, therefore, actually *is* optional if those circumstances don't apply to you.

Because law schools really do want to give you the opportunity to provide all the information you deem important, they also give you that chance when the deadline is past—through the wait-list letter. All these crucial secondary documents are the subject of this chapter.

ARE OPTIONAL ESSAYS OPTIONAL?

The bottom-line question, "Should you write an optional essay?" has one answer: "Yes." Yale Law is on record as stating that the vast majority of its successful applicants treat the optional essay as required, and more than a few applicants placed on admissions hold at top law schools have been pointedly "invited" to submit the optional essays they initially ignored—and were then promptly admitted.

Banish the idea that optional essays should only be used if you have extenuating circumstances—like bad grades—to explain away. As we'll see later in this chapter, those narrow and often negative topics are actually ideal for the addendum. As for the argument that the optional essay will only turn an impatient and bleary-eyed adcom against you, the truth is it might—but only if you write a rambling, off-the-cuff, valueless porridge of an essay. Committees may be overworked, but they're also professionals who like nothing more than discovering qualified and distinctive applicants who show their enthusiasm by taking every opportunity to make their case. Just as visiting the campus a second time communicates your intense interest in a school, the optional essay signals that you are willing to expend extra effort to win admission. After plowing through dozens of applications that seem casually tossed off (or, worse, don't even bother to get the school's name right), your "extra effort" will help you stand out from the pack. Take every advantage you can.

Moreover, deciding to take law schools up on their offer to treat these essays as optional can send the unprepossessing message that you have only a limited number of accomplishments or distinctive experiences to share. Submitting a good optional essay sends the message: "There's more where this came from. I've done a lot!" And if you're top-tier law school material, you really ought to have new and important material to add.

The Open-Ended Optional Essay

As with the personal statement, the subject matter of the optional essay is often left up to you, though schools usually suggest several topics to guide you. In addition to its required personal statement, for example, Boston University invites you to "provide information regarding your ethnic, cultural, or family background that is relevant to your development. You may also choose to discuss particular achievements, including obstacles overcome, that have not already been addressed in this application." Similarly, New York University encourages you to "provide any information," but then offers a range of topics, from the negative (such as LSAT scores and grades) to subjects with potentially positive impact on your admissions chances (like disabilities or a "personal/family history of educational or socioeconomic disadvantage").

This open-endedness with suggested positive and negative topics is the standard model for most of the optional essays you'll encounter. But why on earth devote the precious real estate of an optional essay to issues that can only hurt you—like weak LSATs—when you could shovel those into an addendum and focus your optional essay on powerful stories that might mitigate your negatives? So ignore schools' invitations to discuss grades, test scores, criminal incidents, and the like in your optional essay. Use it proactively.

The open-endedness of most optional essays is fortunate for you because it minimizes the strategizing you must do when deciding how to divide all your stories between a personal statement and the optional essay. As a rule of thumb, you should focus your personal statement on your strongest material (most distinctive, most impressive, most recent, etc.) and relegate the rest to your optional essay. In other words, if you have a powerful story about overcoming adversity, don't sideline it in your optional essay unless you have a very good reason to. Lead with your best in the personal statement, and devote your optional essay to your unused positive material: why you need a law degree, perhaps, or your best academic or professional accomplishment, or a distinctive hobby or extracurricular activity.

So what exactly should you write about? One way to answer this is to return to the self-marketing "handle" we discussed in Chapter 1—the two- or three-theme message you've been trying to convey across your application. If you were thorough in your initial "data-mining" step, you should have more stories than can reasonably be told in one personal statement and optional essay. When both the personal statement and optional essay have open-ended topics, as they usually do, you can allocate your stories across these two essays so they communicate all your themes and make your case in the way that's most effective for you.

Perhaps you intended to discuss the weekly advice column you write for the *Quincy Herald* but couldn't fit it into the available topics. Your optional essay could be the place to highlight this unusual, creative hobby. Work-related stories can also work as optional essays; just be sure they really add value. If you work in an unusual industry and haven't had a chance to communicate what makes it distinctive, enjoyable, or challenging in the personal statement, then the optional essay is your chance. Perhaps you're trying to offset your lack of managerial roles by emphasizing your leadership skills. In that case, your optional essay could dramatize a work situation in which you worked subtly behind the scenes to build momentum for a key decision. Or it could focus on your rise through the ranks at your local Toastmasters. International experiences that show you expanding your sense of self, a part-time business you started out of your garage, running for local political office or serving in the military, even what you've learned about multiculturalism as a participant in a cross-cultural relationship—the range of possible uses is enormous.

Since the optional essay represents your last chance to market yourself to the admissions committee and you don't want to outstay your welcome, avoid writing about prosaic academic or workplace accomplishments or "football hero" type essays. Look for that one remaining story that only you can tell that will deepen the committee's sense that you are a distinctive person of many "parts." The more outside the box your story or insights are, the more benefit you may gain. Many a law school applicant has experienced the power of choosing an unusual topic when a dean mentions the essay months later—or even reads it to the whole entering class. So long as you stay within bounds, you should choose quirky over safe.

As we saw in Chapter 2, law schools also love "overcoming hardship" stories. They love to hear "come-from-behind" tales in which you (the hero) show your fortitude and character by redeeming yourself in the closing minutes. Failure → understanding → redemption is a traditional pattern in all story-telling; you can use it in this essay to arouse the reader's interest and sympathy. Indeed, if your "obstacles overcome" story was strong, ideally you worked it into your personal statement. If that wasn't possible or you have more than one such tale, the optional essay is the perfect place.

Another use for the optional essay is to drive home your desire to attend your target school. Space limitations may have prevented you from doing more than quickly surveying the school's virtues in the personal statement. In the optional essay, you could portray your "fit" in a more personal and focused way by, say, narrating your recent campus visit, talking about the alumnus who is your role model, or spelling out your plan for starting a student club.

Law schools are also partial to leadership stories because initiative, drive, and interpersonal skills are key traits of effective lawyers. Don't assume that leadership can only mean "telling people what to do" in formal management situations. You don't have to occupy positions of great formal authority or work in huge and diverse groups to impress schools with your leadership. You do have to show that you have given serious thought to what leadership really means and have found ways to demonstrate it.

On the broadest level, leadership simply means assuming personal ownership of something in a group situation in order to create a positive result that would not have occurred without you. "In a group" is essential; on some level your leadership example must show you influencing the actions of others. At a minimum, then, leadership implies initiative; doing "more" than others; inspiring; being proactive, not reactive. So, starting with college, put the microscope to all your group experiences—work, academic, extracurricular, community, personal—as we did in Chapter 1. Ask questions like these:

■ Can you think of a time when you were specifically praised for your leadership skills?

■ Have you ever been elected by a group of people for a position of responsibility?

- What methods do you use to motivate people?

- Do you have a philosophy of leadership? Has it changed over time?

- Have people ever followed your lead?

- Have you persuaded others to pursue a certain course of action?

Follow these questions wherever they lead. Because most applicants are still relatively low on the professional totem pole, their best leadership examples may well come from community, academic, or personal activities. Indeed, community leadership can often be more impressive than professional leadership because you're leading volunteers who don't have to follow you (or even be there) and frequently interacting with people at a more senior level than you would be at work.

Your leadership essay will need to inform readers what obstacles you faced—these should stem from people issues. Perhaps you were new to a project, two of your teammates were feuding, a new-hire's learning curve was steeper than expected, or the client-side manager seemed to have walked right out of a *Dilbert* strip. Whatever the challenge, emphasize the differences and issues between people, not the functional loggerheads and technical hurdles. Turn it into a human-interest story from the start.

Next, show how you addressed each of these leadership challenges by deploying your leadership skills. Think in terms of both traits and tactics. What three leadership traits or qualities did you show in helping the group rise to the challenge? What were the tactical steps you took to overcome people issues? They don't have to be epochal. Taking the time to listen to a teammate or changing your personal style to steer around differences (cultural, functional, gender, age, or racial, etc.) with another teammate are worth mentioning. Always describe the small human-level things you did to assuage egos, show gratitude, move people forward. These are the details that (together with the lessons learned) make leadership essays work. Show the school through mini-examples *how* you lead—inclusively? intuitively? analytically?

Law schools will also want to see you step back from your leadership story and give evidence that you learned from experience. Many applicants will slot in a few deep-sounding sentences here and call it a night. Instead, you must show how such leadership lessons stem organically from the details of your story. This will show that you are reflective and self-aware about leadership, that you have thought about what leadership means, and that you are conscious of how to practice it.

Whether you write about a leadership story, personal challenge, or your passion for collecting thirteenth-century Persian religious icons, take full advantage of the freedom of the optional essay to wow the admissions committee with your multidimensional self.

The Assigned-Topic Optional Essay

A second type of optional essay assigns a specific topic. If you choose to submit this essay, then it must be about that topic. The two most common required topics are—surprise—diversity and personal disadvantage. Duke's optional essay topic is typical of the former:

> Because we believe diversity enriches the educational experience of all our students, Duke Law School seeks to admit students from different academic, cultural, social, ethnic, and economic backgrounds. If you choose to submit this essay, tell us how you think you would contribute to the intellectual and social life of the law school.

Some permutation of this can be found in the applications of a long list of schools. In part, this diversity obsession is because landmark events like the Supreme Court's *Hopwood v. Texas* decision and California's Proposition 209 have discouraged or prevented law schools from maintaining different LSAT and GPA minimums for minority applicants. As a result, adcoms must fulfill their mission to offer equal educational opportunity by looking more closely at minority applicants' qualitative qualifications—as glimpsed in the essays. Some schools only require diversity statements from applicants who define themselves as underrepresented minorities:

> Do you believe that your admission would help to correct the traditional under-representation of a particular minority or disadvantaged group in the legal profession? If yes, . . . explain why you believe that group to be underrepresented and describe how you would work to correct this underrepresentation. [University of Cincinnati]

A much larger number of schools allow you to respond to these optional essays with your own definition of diversity. Use this leeway to your advantage by writing an optional essay that shows that you will add to the diversity of your class in multiple ways, whether through your extracurricular involvements, profession, religious beliefs, family background, or skills—whatever captures your uniqueness.

As with diversity, optional essays that require you to write about disadvantage can be narrow in focus:

> Do you believe you were raised in an economically disadvantaged household? If yes, explain why on a separate sheet of paper. [USC]

Most schools define disadvantage broadly, however, as in "physical, economic, cultural, linguistic, or educational obstacles." Either way, you will want to revisit our discussion in Chapter 2 on essays about overcoming obstacles to identify the come-from-behind stories that (1) show you have earned the opportunity that law school provides and (2) demonstrate the determination and focus needed to prevail that successful attorneys share.

Naturally, for schools that require you to focus your optional essay on diversity or disadvantage, you will need to make sure you are not using material that might help you more in your personal statement. As mentioned earlier, the best rough guideline is to use your personal statement to tell your strongest stories—whatever they are. If your diversity or disadvantage story is your most effective, it may do you the most good in your personal statement because it gives you the most space, and adcoms read it first and approach it with the assumption that this is what you most want them to know. However, even if diversity or disadvantage were key themes in your personal statement, you may still find you have enough unused examples of it to write an effective optional essay on this topic.

The author of samples 17 and 26, a personal statement and a diversity statement, respectively, faced just this dilemma. An African American who rose to success from an unpromising childhood in a Chicago suburb, he could have focused his personal statement on his powerful "obstacles overcome" story and then devoted his diversity statement to nonracial diversity material—such as his unusual background as a violinist or his distinctive profile as a defense industry technologist with security clearance. Instead, he chose to focus his personal statement on his "why the law?" story (a legal battle with the buyer of his condo) so he could use his story as a successful minority member in the diversity essay. Though this violates the "Lead with Your Strongest Story" rule, it was probably a shrewd move. This applicant's minority status was going to help him no matter *where* he described it and, as an older applicant with a nontraditional prelaw career, he needed to establish the seriousness of his interest in the law— his lawsuit story did just that. The bottom line is: the only inflexible rule is that all the stories you feel you must tell find their way into one of your essays.

Diversity and disadvantage topics are not the only ones you may encounter in assigned-topic optional essays, of course. Applicants to Alabama have been invited to write about a life-altering moment; candidates at Pepperdine have been asked to comment on their contribution, given that school's religious affiliation. A fair number of schools devote optional essays to pinning down applicants' reasons for choosing their programs: "Briefly discuss your specific interest in Northwestern University School of Law." For these schools, you will want to use your "why our school?" material (see Chapter 2) in the optional essay and focus your personal statement on other topics.

Use this same mix-and-match approach to address topics like William & Mary's optional essay on an event you're "especially proud" of. This is really just a version of the accomplishment topic that we discussed in Chapter 2. You could therefore insert your best accomplishment material here, and thus free up your personal statement for another mission-critical topic—your diversity profile, your distinctive strengths, or your journey to the law.

Finally, a number of schools offer optional essay topics that seek insights into your intellectual or thoughtful side. Examples include Duke's essay on a subject that has "engaged you intellectually," the University of Buffalo's on two books, Loyola Marymount's on "research you have performed," and Brooklyn Law's on "a course, academic project, book, or cultural experience that has especially enriched your education." Showing off your ability to describe and analyze some intellectual subject will give schools some of the insight they seek here. But a much more effective approach is to use your subject as a way of talking about yourself. (Buffalo hints at this when it warns "This is not a book report.") Instead of spending the entire essay dutifully explaining the ins and outs of your thesis on Wilkie Collins or the plot of *The Color Purple*, step back and explicitly connect the book or subject to your life. Why is it important to you? How did it change you personally or affect your goals? What has it taught you about life or yourself? Make sure your essay answers these questions.

The takeaway here is that even essays that are ostensibly about something or someone else should really be about you. Keep this in mind when tackling a topic like Notre Dame's "What circumstances, events, individuals or institutions have influenced you and how?" If you chose to focus on an individual who has influenced you, the individual you choose will be telling schools a great deal: who you esteem (and thus what you value in others, in yourself, and in life), how you establish and sustain productive relationships (when the individual is someone you've known, that is), and whether you are the kind of person who is flexible enough to respond to another's influence and leadership. Without knowing anything else about someone, we know a lot just learning that one person's hero is Nelson Mandela, another's is Britney Spears, and a third's is his church's youth counselor. What each applicant does with those choices can, of course, be sublime or ridiculous, but the self-revelation is inescapable.

More effective than focusing a "role model" essay on a historical or celebrity figure whom you don't know is to choose a hero or role model from your own life, such as your boss or mentor—people whose personal inspiration you've actually witnessed, rather than just read about. Whomever you choose, the focus of the essay must remain you! Discuss the two or three qualities you admire most in this person, with just enough background context to orient the reader. But avoid the most obvious traits like leadership and determination. Dig deeper. Then, as soon as possible, shift the focus from Joe Role Model to you. What is your personal history with this person? What aspects of his or her personality have you emulated? Which have you rejected and why? What lessons has this person's life offered you? Build your essay around answers to these questions. The heart of this kind of essay, in other words, is not a hagiography of your role model. It is the examples from your own life that illustrate how you apply the lessons you gained from him or her.

Though the specific topics some schools assign in optional essays may make you groan, resist the temptation to leave them unanswered. Think of optional essays as mandatory. And look on the bright side—if you know you have to write about a significant accomplishment in an optional essay, that's at least one less topic you have to worry about fitting into your personal statement.

Multiple Optional Essays

A handful of law schools offer multiple optional essays that force you to strategically spread your stories across a range of topics. For example, in addition to a standard open-ended personal statement, Michigan offers you your choice of two of seven defined topics:

- *Essay 1.* Say more about your interest in the University of Michigan Law School. What do you believe that Michigan has to offer to you and you to Michigan?
- *Essay 2.* Describe your current hopes for your career after completing law school. How will your education, experience, and development to date support those plans?
- *Essay 3.* If you do not think that your academic record or standardized test scores accurately reflect your ability to succeed in law school, please tell us why.
- *Essay 4.* Describe a failure or setback on your life. How did you overcome it? What, if anything, would you do differently if confronted with this situation again?
- *Essay 5.* Describe an experience you've had that speaks to the problems and possibilities of diversity in an educational or work setting.
- *Essay 6.* What do you think are the skills and values of a good lawyer? Which do you already possess? Which do you hope to develop?
- *Essay 7.* How might your background and experience enhance the diversity of our student body or of the legal profession? You might discuss perspectives or experiences relating to socioeconomic disadvantage, disability, race, ethnicity, national origin, age, gender, sexual orientation, or religious affiliation. You might also discuss atypical career goals, employment history, educational background, or special talents or skills.

The challenge here is that you must have enough strong material to spread over three essays (the personal statement and two optionals) without repeating any of your stories. For example, suppose you have a powerful story about overcoming racial or socioeconomic obstacles that you decide to highlight in your personal statement. In this case, you will probably need to focus your two optional essays on the law-related topics (1, 2, or 6). Conversely, suppose you decide to make your Michigan personal statement a standard goals essay: why you chose the law, why Michigan, and what your post-JD goals are. Then, you'll want to avoid Michigan optional topics 1 and 2 (since you've already answered them), and instead devote your optional essays to more personal and self-revealing topics, such as topics 5 or 7 (on diversity) and topic 4 (a failure or setback). Be strategic.

Since Michigan is not the only school that invites you to discuss a failure or setback, let's examine the possibilities and pitfalls of this tricky topic for a moment. Why do law schools suggest this topic? On one level, the failure topic enables adcoms to understand how you analyze difficult situations. Your ability to admit and coolly dissect a personal blunder evinces maturity and humility, qualities law schools value. On another level, failures are classic obstacles, and, as we've seen, how you overcome difficulty says a lot about your character, resilience, and willingness to change in response to the feedback reality gives you. Unfortunately, most applicants tend to react to failure topics like cornered ferrets, defensively denying that they could be anything less than flawless. They avoid the failure topic like it's radioactive and thus miss an opportunity to set themselves apart from other applicants.

If you do have the moxie to take on a failure topic, make sure your story passes the following four-part test:

1. It was clearly your fault because you, for example, let someone down, conspicuously and unexpectedly failed to achieve a reasonable goal, or misread or reacted incorrectly to a situation.

2. It sheds light on an activity or experience not treated elsewhere in your application.

3. It is no more than five years old, but is not so recent that you haven't yet applied the lessons it taught you.

4. It reflects some positive aspect of your personality, such as initiative.

The failure itself, however, is perhaps the least important section of the essay. At least as critical are your analysis of the failure, the lessons it taught you, and the ways you applied those lessons later on. You need to state objectively and succinctly what you did wrong and why, showing the reader how conscientiously and exhaustively you examined this "educational episode." Avoid banal, generalized lessons like, "I learned that leadership means taking responsibility for your mistakes." Much better are lessons like failing to turn to others for help; failing to listen; mishandling stress, conflict, or team dynamics; delaying a decision until you had more data; or failing to correlate ideal objectives with hard realities. Then conclude the essay on a positive note by showing how you applied the lessons you learned to redeem yourself.

Law schools that, like Michigan, ask for a personal statement and multiple optional essays will obviously require extra work on your part, but perhaps not as much as you think. While writing your basic personal statement for other schools, you were probably forced to condense several of your best stories, lopping off key details or abridging "lessons learned." In a sense, multiple-essay schools give you the opportunity to reinsert that material, provided it's still somewhere on your cutting-room floor. If you're lucky, you may only need to dig through earlier drafts of your personal statement to find content that, with some retooling and polishing, is ready to use.

THE FINE ART OF DAMAGE CONTROL: ADDENDA

Some law schools invite you to include "extenuating circumstance" topics like grades and test scores in the optional essay, and sometimes even in the personal statement itself. As we noted earlier, you should avoid doing this. Even these schools will almost always accept an "addendum" or "separate statement" in addition to the personal statement and optional essay. It's far better to bunch your negative material in one brief separate sheet than to blunt your case by mixing your exculpatory explanations in with your positive message, using up space you could have spent deepening your marketing effort.

If an explanation of a negative is necessary, the addendum is the best place to air it. The two most common ways of doing damage control are (1) making the case, with evidence, that what appears to be a weakness really isn't and (2) acknowledging the weakness but building the case that you've grown past it. The difference between a weak explanation and a compelling one is more than fancy wording. If your reason for botching the LSAT is flimsy, don't expect nimble-footed prose to gloss it all over. Better to avoid the addendum altogether. In contrast, if your reasons reflect complex factors or circumstances beyond your control, you should exploit the opportunity that the addendum offers you.

Addenda brevity is most definitely the soul of wit. Short one- or two-paragraph statements will usually enable you to go into all the detail that's likely to do you any good. Get in and get out fast. Let's look next at the most common addendum topics.

LSAT Scores

Two types of explanations are most commonly given for low LSAT scores. The first is that some extraordinary circumstance occurred just before or during the test session itself that unfairly affected your performance. Such circumstances can range from the obvious—your spouse was hospitalized the night before, you had an auto accident on the way to the test center—to the iffy—you weren't

feeling well during the exam, the testing environment was noisy or too hot or cold, or you weren't able to concentrate for some concrete reason.

The problem with all of them is that they could be made by anyone, they are difficult to substantiate, and, most damningly, you could have canceled your score after the test. You should not therefore expect the committee to "excuse" your disappointing score for any of these reasons. They are only worth explaining in an addendum if you later managed a significantly higher score. Because many law schools average all your LSAT scores, your lower score can live to haunt you so make your explanation one that will persuade the adcoms to cut you some slack.

Explanations such as you were working too hard supporting your sick mother to afford a Kaplan LSAT prep course will hold no water. You should have known that LSATs are critical to the admissions decision and given them the highest priority.

The one explanation that may actually help you overcome a disappointing LSAT score is that there has always been a disconnect between your standardized tests scores and your academic performance. If accurate, this may indicate that you are a member of that small minority whose intellectual aptitude is simply not accurately measured by tests like the LSAT, GRE, or SAT. Note that this "outlier" defense will only work if you can point to a clear pattern of standardized test scores that seem to bear no relation to your high grades. For example, you scored a cumulative 900 on your SATs but were National Honor Society and class valedictorian. Obviously, this argument applies to very few applicants; don't attempt it if you're unsure you're one of them.

Remember also that being disappointed with your LSAT score doesn't necessarily justify devoting an addendum to it. If you got a 172 and the school's median is 173, don't bother.

Poor Grades

Law school adcoms are much more willing to take into account explanations for anomalies in academic transcripts than in LSATs. But this will depend on the magnitude and nature of the anomaly. Some applicants think they should write an addendum to do "damage control" on the lone C they suffered in freshman-year basket weaving. These minor lapses are too trivial to waste space on. Other applicants delude themselves that explanations (even strong ones) can compensate for multiple Fs on a transcript or a long slow downward spiral over four years of college. These "anomalies" may simply be too egregious for the adcoms to overlook. However, if your GPA lapse was marked but not horrific, if it was of limited duration, and if its cause was a specific event or situation (a family matter or a strange grading policy, for example), then a brief explanatory addendum may help.

What explanations for poor grades carry weight? A weak but all-too-common one is the "lack of focus" argument. This only begs the question—why did you have a lack of focus? It's one thing if you struggled because you're the first person in your family to go to college and simply needed time to adjust or you picked the wrong major and so struggled through a few tough classes. It's quite another if you devoted your freshman year to becoming your frat's unofficial kegger king.

The best explanations emphasize concrete factors, preferably those outside your control. If you had unusual and unavoidable family obligations or had to work full-time to self-fund your education, admissions officers will surely cut you slack (though whether they'll admit you is another matter).

Whatever your reasons may be, explain them succinctly, objectively, and maturely. Take responsibility, draw a lesson from the episode, and then state what you've done since to prove that the disappointing grades actually were an anomaly. Note, for example, how the author of the addendum in sample 28 admits that his college extracurricular involvements were "excessive," but takes care to remind the reader of the variety and impeccable caliber of these involvements. To underscore that his undergraduate grades were truly an anomaly, he then devotes a second brief paragraph to characterizing his outstanding academic record in rigorous graduate programs. There's no whining or prevaricating, just impressive facts.

The effectiveness of your addendum's explanations for disappointing grades may also be affected by your performance on the LSAT (and vice versa). That is, if your LSAT score is high enough to help the school rise in the national rankings, the adcoms may be willing to cut you slack for a less-than-competitive GPA.

Bar Examiner Issues

Law schools are part of the process by which bar examiners on Character and Fitness Committees police the ethical integrity of professionals seeking licenses to practice law in their states. Law school deans are required to submit an affidavit or evaluation of your moral fitness to practice the law to these panels. Their endorsement of you will depend on your response to questions that appear on every law school's application. These tend to fall into four general categories:

- *Undergraduate misdeeds.* This includes any incidents of probation, suspension, or dismissal either for disciplinary (stupid frat pranks) or academic reasons (poor performance). These usually will not be deal-breakers, but cheating, plagiarism, vandalism, or worse are very serious matters indeed.

- *Previous law school enrollment.* Did you graduate? If you did, why do you want another law degree? If you didn't, under what circumstances did you leave?

- *Separation from an employer or the military for negative reasons.* This includes anything other than an honorable discharge from the military and any scenario in which you left an employer because *it* wanted you to go.

- *Criminal incidents.* This usually includes any and all "brushes with the law," except minor traffic violations, regardless of their final disposition, including disorderly conduct, drunk driving, shoplifting, and speeding, and regardless of when in your life they occurred.

Two issues are at stake in your responses to such questions: the severity of and circumstances surrounding any affirmative answers you give and your ability to honestly admit such incidents.

The worst thing you can do is to deny an incident. Law school adcoms and bar examiners have seen it all, and you might be surprised at the kinds of backgrounds that are sometimes green-lighted for admission. You could wind up being denied admission to the bar for disclaiming an incident that they would have overlooked. So long as your situation is not too egregious, has a reasonable explanation, and reflects a behavior that is now demonstrably in your past, then adcoms (and later bar examiners) may well decide to give you a shot at redemption. Anything suggesting a pattern of such behavior, however, may close the door on your law career.

Stick to describing the facts as objectively as you can. Leave nothing important out, but don't appear to offer excuses, whine, or blame others. This is not the place to exercise your talent for spin, hair-splitting, or subtle verbal glosses (earn your JD and you'll have plenty of opportunities for that). The sin here, in other words, is not only false answers but misleading or incomplete ones. If you are concerned that your past mistakes are serious enough, check directly with the bar examiner's board of the state you intend to practice in.

Other Extenuating Circumstances

The range of weaknesses that applicants may need to discuss in the addendum is not limited to grades, scores, and personal integrity issues, of course. If you're unemployed, for example, you may want to use the addendum to explain what you've been doing with your time. Provide mini-stories about the activities that have been occupying you since the pink slip, such as classes or community involvements. As mentioned, however, if you are unemployed because your organization asked you to leave, you must also explain the incidents surrounding your termination or departure.

The impact of visa restrictions on career plans, an abbreviated stay in medical or business school, a transcript showing more than three universities or a six-year undergraduate career, reasons for deferring admission a year ago—all of these raise concerns that the addendum can alleviate. Less typically, the addendum can help you make the case that, for example, being wheelchair-bound is not an impediment or that the clinical depression you suffered in college is a thing of the past. The bottom line is the same: schools offer addenda not to torpedo your application but to give you a chance to explain negatives honestly, succinctly, and positively.

CLOSING ARGUMENTS: WAIT-LIST LETTERS

Wait-list letters represent one final opportunity law schools give you to make your case for admission, one you hopefully will never need. If you do, it means you're in a peculiar admissions purgatory whose duration you may have no way of controlling. Whether you ever see the Pearly Gates of acceptance will usually depend on the unpredictable characteristics of the applicant pool you're competing against.

But that doesn't mean you must simply passively wait and hope. You must adopt a positive and proactive attitude—there's really no alternative. First, realize that the wait-list letter means you qualified for admission. Congratulations. You are probably on the wait list because they have already admitted applicants with your profile and want diversity in the class. Or they found your qualifications impressive, but found someone else's even more so. The point is, they believe you can handle their program; they just ran out of spaces. Who gets pulled off the wait list may therefore come down to subjective factors, such as demonstrated enthusiasm.

What can you do to enhance your chances of being plucked off the list when a space opens up? For the resourceful and strategic, even purgatory represents an opportunity. Do you have what it takes to convince the school that you really belong there more than anywhere else? It is the motivated applicants—the ones who create and execute a sustained and enthusiastic wait-list campaign—who get in more often than any others.

The wait list (or "reserve" list as it's sometimes called) is simply an administrative yield-management tool. It enables schools to achieve their targeted class size by letting in wait-listed applicants to compensate for the applicants who've turned down their offers of admission. Naturally, law schools with high yields (say, 85 percent) will need to rely on the wait list less than will schools who matriculate only half (or less) of the applicants they admit. You must accept the fact from the outset that, in law school wait lists, many are called but few are chosen. The odds will be stacked against you.

Some schools may review their wait lists as often as every week. Others will wait until the end of the admissions season in late spring. Some schools periodically remove wait-listed candidates who they no longer believe have a chance of eventually gaining admission. Final wait-list decisions can be made by the admissions director him- or herself or by the admissions staff as a whole. They typically occur in the late spring or summer (though sometimes as late as the first day of class) when schools finally know who will be accepting and who won't.

Some law schools rank their wait-listees in some fashion, such as by the index number (LSAT + GPA) assigned by the Law School Data Assembly Service. Some of these schools establish priority and nonpriority wait lists, others separate wait lists for in-state and out-of-state applicants, still others use wait lists strictly to fill out the statistical diversity of their classes. If you ask politely, some schools may tell you where you stand on the wait list and how many wait-listees have historically been admitted. The more rigid the ranking mechanism, the less a proactive wait-list campaign will improve your chances. But it certainly can never hurt and, for schools that do not rank wait-listees, your campaign may win you admission.

Wait-List Letters: What to Do

Seize the initiative and launch a wait-list campaign. Unless the school completely discourages further contact, take a proactive approach. If the school encourages contact, do so. In fact, even if it doesn't encourage contact but simply says it is "allowed" or "can't hurt," you have all the green light you need. Map a strategy of regular, but not overzealous, contacts that will keep you on the radar while demonstrating your enthusiasm for and fit with the school's program and culture. The exact particulars of your campaign will vary depending on the school and exactly when you are put on the wait list, but it can include letters, additional visits to the school, an offer to interview, letters of support from others, and occasional phone calls.

Your first step is to closely follow the instructions provided in the letter advising you of your wait-list status. Promptly accept the offer of wait-list limbo in whatever manner the school requires: by note, e-mail, phone, or postcard. Indicate that you will be following up with a full-scale wait-list letter in a few days. If you have not visited the school, do so. Ask for a tour, attend a class (or two), meet with students. If you have already visited, do it again. The farther you live from the wait-listing school, the more impressive your gesture of a visit (or revisit) will be.

Develop a practical plan for visiting the school and see if you can also set up an appointment with a member of the admissions committee. You probably won't get a formal interview (unless perhaps someone you know can pull strings for you), but you may get an informal meeting where you can pose questions to an adcom—a great opportunity to make an impression. During your visit, also go to the student union and strike up conversations with students wherever you find them. Learn what you can. After the visit, send a thank-you note to whomever you spoke with. In the note, reiterate your interest in the school and show how the visit was valuable in confirming that interest.

Within a few days of your initial acceptance of the school's wait-list offer, send out a one-page—but certainly no longer than two-page—letter. You have already shown that you qualify for the school; otherwise you wouldn't find yourself on the wait list. Now give the adcom additional reasons to admit you. Address the letter to the wait-list contact person designated by the school. If no name was provided, address the letter to the person who notified you of your wait-list status or, failing that, to the Admissions Director.

The wait-list letter should have roughly five parts: an introduction, a section reaffirming your fit with the school, a section on recent developments, a section addressing possible weaknesses in your application, and a conclusion.

The Introduction

Tell them why you are writing: to formally accept wait-list status. Thank them effusively for continuing to keep your life and future suspended in uncertainty. Ruthlessly expunge any notes of disappointment or ambivalence. This introduction should establish a positive, optimistic, grateful tone. It should also directly and succinctly state the topics to be addressed in the letter, namely, your reaffirmation of your fit with the school, your updates on developments in your career and life since you applied, and your efforts to compensate for the weaknesses you perceive in your application. Your introductory paragraph might also inform the reader that you've included an additional letter of recommendation from a new recommender who will add a fresh perspective on your candidacy.

The Body: Reaffirm School Fit

Reinforce your commitment to and interest in the school's program, but do it in an original way. For example, feel free to mention how the school's philosophy and resources match your educational preferences and goals, but don't just cut and paste from your personal statement or essays. Reword your original material or, better yet, cite new examples. For example, demonstrate how your recent visit confirmed and deepened your interest in the program. Perhaps you sat in on a class (which one? who taught it? what were your impressions?) or chatted up some 3Ls in the cafeteria (what were their names? what did they say? what did you like about them?). Or perhaps your work or research interests have recently led you to explore a faculty member's work or touched on the mission of one of the school's clinical programs. If so, deliberately and specifically flesh out the bridge between your work or research interest and that faculty member or program. They do want to know if there are real affinities between you and their school.

Does your letter demonstrate the qualities of the school that wait-listed you? For a wait-list letter to the University of Pennsylvania, have you emphasized such Penn strengths as high student satisfaction and rich cross-disciplinary opportunities? For a Yale wait-list letter, does your commitment to public interest law shine out from every example? Notice how the writer of the short-but-sweet wait-list letter in sample 31 uses her acceptance by American University's School of International Service to subtly pressure American University's Law School to make a positive decision. It worked.

The Body: Recent Developments

Inform the school of new achievements, initiatives, and developments in your life. Give them more reasons to admit you. Show them you're an even stronger applicant than you were five months ago. For law school applicants still in college, this could mean recent grades or academic work. For older applicants, this could be promotions, new leadership roles at or outside work, or skills acquired on the job. Did you have a 4.0 GPA during the last quarter? Have you led a project or organization? Volunteered? Have you taken your department, business, or club in a new direction? Have you had an article published? Launched a business? Assumed additional responsibility? Succeeded in a particularly demanding class or project? All can be effective fodder for a wait-list letter.

In short, mention any recent accomplishments that you did not discuss in your application and, ideally, tie them back to some of the themes or experiences you raised in your personal statement. If you don't have promotions or even partic-ularly notable achievements, don't fret. Basically, anything new that has occurred in your professional or community life since you applied can—if you analyze it— be presented as a development that has strengthened your candidacy (though never try to exaggerate a nonaccomplishment into an accomplishment).

Demonstrate that you are an even stronger applicant than when you applied, and the school may draw the logical conclusion that you are as deserving as the candidates who have already been admitted.

The Body: Addressing Concerns

Read the school's wait-list notification letter for any hints of deficiency in your profile. Some schools will tell wait-listees of their concerns or issues in the wait-list notification—for example, recommending explicitly that you retake the LSAT. Some schools will simply invite you to contact them, and your contact person will sometimes supply quite specific and helpful advice. Of course, other schools will leave you entirely in the dark. But even in these cases it's usually possible to arrive on your own at some idea of what's holding you back. For example, it's easy enough to find out if your LSAT score is below the school's average—if so, consider retaking it. The vast majority of application deficiencies involve poor numbers (LSAT and/or GPA), inadequate emphasis on what makes the applicant's profile or potential contribution unique, insufficient community or extracurric-ular involvement, or poorly demonstrated interest in the school. Evaluate your application closely to see whether any of these deficiencies pertain.

If you're still on the wait list when your final semester grades are posted, get that transcript into the school's hands as soon as possible (assuming they're good!). If you are not accepted, those grades will help you when you reapply in the fall. If you suspect your relatively weak history of community involvement is the major reason a school has wait-listed you, explain how deeply involved you've been in your law firm's pro bono project over the past four months. In other words, whatever your perceived shortcomings are, address them—without bringing undue attention to them.

Keep your wait-list letter short and sweet—two pages maximum. Don't succumb to the temptation to rewrite or even summarize your life history or personal statement. Stay focused on what you have accomplished since applying, the school fit issue, and your perceived weaknesses.

The Conclusion

Your conclusion should repeat the gratitude and enthusiasm themes of the introduction (without using the same language). You could also, space permitting, briefly recap the three or four contributions or uniqueness factors you believe you can bring to the school. If you are certain you would attend this school, make it clear that it is your first choice and that you will immediately and enthusiastically accept an offer of admission. A few attractive applicants are sometimes wait-listed because the law school doubted they would actually accept an offer of admission. In these cases, simply informing them that you will come may release you from wait-list limbo.

If you are not enclosing an additional letter of recommendation, but one is on the way, let the school know who will be sending it and perhaps even what aspects of your application he or she will shed light on. Perhaps assure the school that if there is anything you can do to improve your candidacy, you are happy to do it. You may want to express your willingness to provide any additional information the committee needs. Definitely thank them for their time.

After the Wait-List Letter

As important as it is, the wait-list letter is just the beginning. As soon as you learn you're on the wait list, you also need to dust off any unused letters of recommendation and ask the recommenders to consider updating them with developments since you applied. If you have no unused letters, you should begin identifying people who can add new, enthusiastic insights on your professional, community, or even personal life. (See Chapter 4 for more on recommendation letters.)

You need, in other words, to enlist your fan club. You could seek additional letters of recommendation from former or current professors or supervisors on and off the job, assuming they didn't write one of the letters of recommendation included in your application. Since your wait-list status is proof that your application has at least one flaw, these additional letters of recommendation offer you a perfect opportunity to have a third party do damage control on this weakness by emphasizing offsetting facts or skills. Remember, these wait-list recommendation letters do not have to be as lengthy as your original letters of recommendation, nor do they have to be written by someone who knows you as well as your original recommenders.

You should also consider soliciting the help of those contacts among current students and alumni of the school that wait-listed you who are convinced or can be convinced to be genuinely enthusiastic about your candidacy. Ask them to call the admissions office on your behalf and/or write brief letters of support (as distinct from full-fledged letters of recommendation), emphasizing how closely you match the program's culture. Of course, you need to know them well enough to ask this huge favor of them, so set aside time to "interview" with them. This will give them a formal period in which to get to know you, evaluate you, and form, hopefully, a positive judgment of you.

These fan letters can talk about your recent professional or community developments, and they can and should emphasize your fit with the wait-listing school. They are best if they come from students and recent alumni. A bigwig can help, but is by no means necessary to do the trick. Whether you enlist the help of traditional recommenders or last-minute insider supporters (or both), try to synchronize their efforts so their letters are arriving at the school, say, two weeks apart. A batch of enthusiastic letters arriving all at once is a waste of goodwill. And, again, observe the school's wait-list instructions. Don't send more letters of recommendation than they allow.

How soon after your initial wait-list letter should you begin sending supplemental letters of support? Generally speaking, three to four weeks later is appropriate. Your check-in phone calls and e-mails can be more frequent, but don't abuse the privilege. If you are still on the wait list, also consider sending a new update or wait-list letter, and perhaps an additional essay as well. Even if you have very little new to relate, do your best to emphasize the new and create a sense of momentum.

The point is never to give up until you absolutely have to. The wait list is the ultimate test of your passion for attending a particular school and of your determination as a future lawyer. The upside of that test is that schools will sometimes respond if that passion and determination is sustained and genuine—and luck is on your side.

CHAPTER

4

Credible Enthusiasm:
Letters of Recommendation

Sometimes the last item read in your file, sometimes treated as a pro forma rubber stamp, occasionally the element that saves or damns your application, the letter of recommendation plays a unique role in the law school admissions process. It is the only element in the application folder in which a party other than you and the school is given the chance to weigh in on your qualifications. Because it is the element over which you have the least control, the letter of recommendation is truly the application wildcard. For that reason, recommendation letters (sometimes called "faculty evaluation," "appraisal of applicant," "letter of evaluation," or "statement of instructor") must not be taken lightly.

A detailed, well-written recommendation from someone who understands the qualities that make for successful law students and lawyers can give your application an imprimatur that's hard to beat. Moreover, since most law schools don't interview applicants, the recommendation letter's role in making your distinctive profile come alive is even more critical. For those applicants who lie in the middle of their target school's application pool, the impact of recommendation letters on their chances for admission can be enormous. This is where a hair breadth's difference often separates one candidate from the next.

A supportive recommender can speak enthusiastically about you in a way that you cannot—at least without sounding like a raving egotist. And, as a more experienced individual with broader exposure, your recommender will have observed aspects of your skills that you aren't likely to see yourself. Bottom line: Recommendation letters can do what no other parts of your application can. Make sure you execute them well.

This chapter differs from every other in that it concerns an application document that schools do *not* want you to write yourself. Yet these same schools also encourage you to proactively help your recommender craft letters that really strengthen your application. This chapter will help you and your recommender do just that.

Let's get started by looking at what law schools use letters of recommendation for and what they hope to find in them.

WHAT DO RECOMMENDATION LETTERS DO ANYWAY?

You may be thinking, "Why all this fuss over documents that arc almost always dripping with praise? How can schools take letters of recommendation seriously?" There's no denying that the vast majority of letters of recommendation are positive endorsements. But consider that a small, but not negligible, fraction of the recommendations schools receive are actually negative—not lukewarm, negative. Add to this the large number of letters that, though ostensibly positive, contain one telltale deal-breaking hint or fail to back up their claims, and you begin to see how much impact a truly enthusiastic and detailed letter can have.

The experienced adcom member knows how to read between the lines—to gauge when a negative remark is a legitimate weakness and when it's a ding trigger, to separate the fulsome praise from the hard accomplishment. The percentage of positive recommendations may be huge, it's true, but there's a much smaller universe of genuinely enthusiastic and knowledgeable recommendations. Not coincidentally, at top schools this universe tends to coincide with the universe of accepted applicants.

Because law schools are not all the same, what constitutes a good letter of recommendation will often differ slightly from school to school. But, in general, schools use letters of recommendation to determine whether you can handle the intellectual boot camp that is law school and then go on to do the school proud practicing law. As we'll see later in this chapter, schools use recommendation letters to evaluate you in three general areas:

1. Your analytical, academic, or intellectual abilities

2. Your writing or communication skills

3. Your character, personal qualities, or personality

Letters of recommendation also serve a corroborative function. They tell the school whether the people who have seen your mind and personality at work view your contribution in the same way you do. Do you possess mature self-knowledge? Did you over-spin your achievements in your personal statement? Recommendation letters provide the reality check. Schools are looking to see if your recommenders also confirm your themes: the self-marketing "handle" you've been pitching across your application.

A recommendation letter that confirms all the factual claims you make but contradicts the spin you've put on them will hurt you. For example, to support his assertion that public interest law is his post-JD goal, Nick's personal statement downplays the specifics of his major in political philosophy as well as his presidency of his college's Libertarian Party and plays up Nick's tutoring and church work. In her letter, Nick's recommender asserts that Nick has unusually sharp analytical, research, and writing skills—just as he claimed. However, she completely fails to back up Nick's social impact message. In fact, she describes how he ran for student government on a "self-reliance" ticket and crafted a brilliant defense of Social Darwinism in his college thesis. Admissions officers, smelling a rat, ease Nick's file into the ding bin. The moral of the story: dissonance between recommender and applicant can be fatal.

On a more subtle level, schools can also use letters of recommendation to gauge whether you (1) know how to read people well enough to discern enthusiastic recommenders from the merely compliant and (2) have the negotiation skills to convince busy recommenders to do you a big favor.

Ask a roomful of admissions officials what they value most in a recommendation letter, and you'll probably hear two words: candor and specifics. They want to know that the recommender is being honest with them and that praise is tempered by objective "data." In other words, they want concrete credibility. Does this really mean that schools will favor an applicant whose recommendations discuss weaknesses over one whose recommendations claim the applicant has none? Yes, it does. No one is perfect, and a recommendation that offers no negative comment loses believability (though, of course, your credibility can also be communicated by specifics and examples).

As you and your recommenders follow the advice contained in this chapter, remember that law schools don't admit applicants because they have no blemishes. They admit them because their positives are so consistently striking and substantial as to outweigh their faults.

HOW LONG?

Generally speaking, the higher your target school lies in the law school food chain, the more likely it will view a long recommendation letter favorably—provided it's meaty. The simple reason for this is that longer letters demonstrate the recommender's enthusiasm.

Though long letters can certainly backfire if they lack examples, are written poorly, or are excessively long, they do tend to show that the recommender thought highly enough of you to take the time out of his or her busy day to write an extensive endorsement. Law schools generally do not place length restrictions on recommendation letters. They want recommenders to feel encouraged to say as much as they choose to. In fact, admissions officers have a dismissive nickname for short letters—"coffee-break recommendations."

So, how long should a recommendation be? Less than one single-spaced page is usually too short; two, and perhaps three, pages are fine; and more than three is usually too long, unless the letter is for an older applicant about whom the recommender has many stories to tell.

HOW MANY?

A handful of law schools do not accept any recommendation letters at all, while a few don't *require* any (though only foolish applicants will read that as an invitation not to submit any). At the other end of the spectrum, some schools require or recommend that you submit up to three and, in one case, even four letters. The typical law school, however, requires two letters and will accept up to four. (Some programs, like New York University's, require an additional letter concerning "commitment to public service" from applicants applying for certain public interest–related scholarships.)

Many applicants decide that at least one additional letter beyond the requirement will add value. You should too. As a rule of thumb, the older you are, the more sense it makes to submit three or more letters.

If you are using the LSAC's Letter of Recommendation Service (many schools require you to), you will only be able to submit four general (non-school-specific) recommendation letters to each school. However, LSAC also lets you submit an unlimited number of school-specific (or "targeted") letters. This means the LSAC won't be standing in your way if you decide to bombard a school with letters. Indeed, schools have been known to receive as many as 30 individual letters from a single applicant! This flood-tide tactic is best avoided, however. It will only make you look flaky or overly aggressive, and it may prompt adcoms to wonder what red flags you're trying to compensate for.

Note that you may intentionally want to collect more letters from recommenders than schools will let you submit. These unused letters may come in handy if you are wait-listed later in the spring.

SELECTING RECOMMENDERS

The question of whom to ask for your recommendations can get complicated, but some rules of thumb will help:

1. Start by asking who knows you best, through direct interaction over a sustained period (ideally, six months or more).

2. Then ask yourself who is likely to provide a truly enthusiastic endorsement.

3. Finally, if you're still in college or within five years of graduation, focus primarily on academic references; if you're more than five years out, focus on professional references.

These "screens" should give you a manageably short list of potential recommenders. Some (lucky) applicants may still find themselves with too many choices, however. One way to winnow the list is to strive for a mix of recommenders that captures the broadest range of your skills, experiences, and themes, thus showing the schools that you possess the well-roundedness they covet. For example, you could choose two professors, an employer, and a supervisor or peer at a community or extracurricular organization. Such breadth will also enable you to minimize the overlap between the stories each recommender tells. (It's no disaster if two recommenders refer to one or two of the same achievements, so long as they provide a different perspective on them.)

In gauging which people from each these categories—academic, professional, extracurricular—will produce the best letters, return constantly to your initial enthusiasm and knowledge "screens": who knows you best and who will write the strongest endorsement. By keeping in mind these three criteria of enthusiasm, direct knowledge of you, and breadth of insight, your chances of identifying the most effective mix of recommenders will be high. In fact, the criteria that law schools really care about—intellectual skills, writing ability, and character—are so broad that three recommenders should be able to provide original slants on your achievements without repeating one another.

If you're shrewd in your choice of recommenders, and they come through for you, you'll have taken a crucial step toward convincing the admissions committee that you deserve a spot. For most applicants, the first step is to secure a letter from a professor.

FIRST LETTER: PROFESSOR

Unless you've been out of school for five years or more, at least one—and for some schools two—of your recommendation letters must come from an undergraduate professor. The reason for this is simple. Law schools' primary concern is whether you can handle the academic white heat of law school, and who better to evaluate your intellectual tools than one of their own—a professor. Are you intellectually gifted? Do you study hard? Do you speak up in class? Can you grow intellectually over time? These questions are what education is all about, so law schools naturally look to educators for the answers. (A small handful of schools, such as University of Houston, Texas University, and University of Wisconsin, are open to nonacademic letters, even for your primary letter.)

Of course, some professors are better sources for these answers than others. Here's an ideal faculty recommender: a well-known professor at a rigorous university, Dr. Kern taught you in three classes in your major (two of them upper level) in which you were always a proactive participant and earned As. Visiting him assiduously during office hours, you developed a mentoring relationship with him and then got to know him even better when you became president of the student club for which Dr. Kern serves as faculty advisor. After your junior year, Dr. Kern hired you as his summer research assistant. After this long and positive relationship, it came as a pleasant surprise when Dr. Kern told you he has written recommendation letters for dozens of successful applicants at top law schools over the years, and he considers you one of the best.

OK, not everyone can develop this kind of relationship with a professor. But many do, and they don't necessarily have to be the sharpest tools in the shed— just the most resourceful. Building long-term relationships with professors takes some foresight as well the ability to do the kind of academic work they will be inspired to speak enthusiastically about. So choose wisely and start early.

If this kind of scenario is not possible, don't panic. Schools will happily "settle" for an enthusiastic letter from any professor who knows you well—even if he or she is outside your major or taught you in a course that doesn't emphasize the skills law schools look for (analytical and writing ability). If you're at a big state school and a teaching assistant you got to know very well will write you a glowing letter, don't even think about substituting it with a letter from a professor who remembers you only as a name on a list and gave you a C.

For some applicants, their undergraduate prelaw advisor will be a logical choice. Because he is often a professor, teaches in a discipline related to the law, understands the law admissions game (through membership in one of the regional prelaw advisors' associations), and has worked with dozens of law school applicants, his evaluation of you will often carry some weight with the admissions committee. But this weight will be substantially undercut if his knowledge of you is limited to the few hours he has interacted with you in his role of prelaw advisor.

If you earned your undergraduate degree five plus years ago, you should still try to get a recommendation from at least one professor, even if you have to work hard to remind her who you are. If you're pushing 30 years old or more, however, not even the most faculty-centric adcoms will expect a letter from an undergraduate professor. They will still want to evaluate your ability to handle law school though. So you will have to encourage your nonacademic recommenders to discuss your intellectual skills and writing ability, even if those skills are not the primary reasons for your success in your current field. For some applicants, one option is to seek a letter from professors who taught them in graduate school.

SECOND LETTER: PROFESSOR OR EMPLOYER

One professor's evaluation of your mind is, for many schools, not enough. They want a second opinion and will only bend this preference for applicants who've been out of school for several years (anywhere from two to eight or more years depending on the school). Law schools' openness to nonacademic recommendations is undoubtedly growing, reflecting law schools' increasing resemblance to business schools in preferring older applicants with work experience. Nevertheless, their preference for faculty letters from younger applicants remains strong and widespread.

Ideally, then, you'll have the same kind of sustained and personal relationship with your second academic recommender as you did with your first. Keep in mind, though, that you don't want rhyming recommendations—letters that say the same things about your skills and performance in quite similar courses. Try to get your second letter from a professor in an entirely different discipline from your first professor. So long as the course tested your analytical, research, and/or reading and writing skills, your performance is relevant to the law schools' concerns. If your most enthusiastic potential recommenders are all in your major, then at least try to find one who can comment on your performance outside the classroom—such as in a student organization—as well as in the classroom.

A small and growing minority of schools are more relaxed about collegiate or recently graduated applicants who use nonacademic recommenders for the second letter. A few schools even prefer that the second letter be nonacademic. So, if you are applying to one of these schools or are an older, nontraditional applicant, whom should you choose to write this second letter? People who can comment on the same criteria as professors—character and intellectual and writing skills.

Lawyers who've seen you operate in a legal context, for example, are a good choice. Aside from their experience in the law and with the qualities that make good lawyers, lawyer recommenders have also (usually) survived law school and are thus in an excellent position to judge whether you can too. This very same familiarity can backfire, however, if the lawyer presumes too much and fills his letter with self-aggrandizing remarks, personal opinions about the law, or retroactive judgments on his law school experience.

If you are applying to law school from a profession outside the law, law schools will prefer a letter from a current boss. He or she is likely to have the seniority and leadership experience to judge employees objectively, and evaluating people is frequently a key part of his or her managerial role. Supervisors' opinions of you thus come with a built-in credibility. A letter from a boss may not always be possible, but it remains an optimal choice for your nonacademic recommenders—unless you've been working for that manager for only six months or so.

If you absolutely cannot get a letter from your current manager, then you should get a letter from another manager at your current employer who knows you well, or from your immediate manager at your most recent employer. Other possibilities include colleagues and peers outside the firm, so long as their relationship to you won't strike the adcoms as compromised. If you're self-employed or work for a family-owned business (note that letters from dad are out), clients, suppliers, or your accountant, lawyer, or venture capitalist can also make good recommendations.

Most older applicants who omit a letter from a current supervisor do so because they don't want to jeopardize their chance for advancement if no law school admits them. Luckily, law schools appreciate the delicacy of this situation, and if you've been with your current employer for under a year, an enthusiastic letter from your previous supervisor is an acceptable alternative, as, of course, is a letter from an academic, provided it isn't too old. In this case, just insert a two-sentence note in your application stating that you're submitting a recommendation from your previous manager or an academic/professor instead.

Another acceptable reason for omitting a letter from a current supervisor is that you are self-employed or work for a family business (since letters from family members don't carry any weight). In these cases, inform the school that you are submitting letters from professors, clients, colleagues, or vendors who can comment authoritatively on your candidacy. If the real reason you've omitted a letter from your current supervisor is that you're unsure he or she would be enthusiastic, simply inform the school that the recommenders you are using are exceptionally well qualified to comment on your performance and potential and back this up with evidence—and leave it at that.

In extraordinary cases, your second letter could come from a supervisor or peer at a community organization or "extracurricular" activity rather than a professor or boss. This is only advisable if your role and performance are unusually strong or the skills you demonstrated in the activity are closely related to the law. Evaluate such extracurricular recommendations this way: if the law school saw only this and your first recommendation letter (as sometimes happens), would the impression the two made be strong enough?

SUBSEQUENT LETTERS

Most applicants submit about three letters, and schools rarely provide guidelines beyond the first two. So you are on your own in deciding whom to get your subsequent letters from. Since your third and subsequent letters are in some sense "extra" letters, you can get a bit creative here and focus more on the rounded portrait of yourself that all your letters together project. That is, a subsequent letter that focuses on a highly defined sliver of your life may still be worthwhile if it balances out the picture of you coming from your primary letters. You want these "extra" letters to come from someone who sheds truly fresh light on your candidacy, whomever that may be. It could be your supervisor at a community organization, for example, especially if your performance or role there was unusually strong or you're applying to a school that views "public interest" applicants favorably.

Coaches, summer employers, advisors in internships, community leaders, or clergy can all be ideal recommenders if they pass the enthusiasm-with-personal-knowledge screen. Provided that your primary recommendations comment specifically on your law school skills—language and research/analytical ability—these subsequent recommenders can focus on helping you stand out from the pack. Try to take advantage of any natural affinities between recommenders and your target schools. For example, a letter from someone you know in the Catholic Church might be a good choice for your application to Catholic University or Notre Dame.

"God" Letters

It should go without saying that procuring a recommendation from a judge, politician, celebrity leader, or higher—the so-called "God" letter—may actually hurt your application if the deity in question doesn't really know you. It should go without saying, but hundreds of law school applicants will do exactly that this year. Don't be one of them. You may think that a VIP recommender's willingness is an exploitable ace in the hole, but such letters are a bad idea for two excellent reasons. First, the VIP recommender is unlikely to know you well enough to say anything that will interest the committee, and, second, your ace-in-the-hole strategy is actually surprisingly common. Schools are inundated by brief, unhelpful letters from VIPs, and some schools have been known to receive an identically worded recommendation from the same politician for several applicants. Rather than waste such "connections" on an empty recommendation, use them to get an interview or to make a call if you get wait-listed.

DEAN'S LETTERS

A holdover from the days when college deans were actually acquainted with their students, the dean's certification is not used by most applicants as a recommendation letter. But it can most definitely serve as one. A function of the law schools' obligation to turn out graduates with sufficient integrity to pass states' "character and fitness" examination, the certification asks deans or other appropriate officials (including your prelaw advisor at some schools) to comment on such matters as your rank in class, your current good standing toward completion of your degree, and any "disciplinary" events such as expulsion, suspension, probation, academic warnings, or even reduced course loads and withdrawals. Some schools use the form to find out if your undergraduate school regarded your standardized test scores as accurate when it admitted you—just in case you claim your LSAT is "nonpredictive." If you do have such administrative black marks, make sure that the dean's certification isn't the only place in your application where they are discussed.

Most dean's certification forms attempt to allay applicants' anxiety by assuring them that the dean does not need to know them in order to fill out the form. How is it possible then to use the dean's form as a letter of recommendation? By positioning yourself to take advantage of the space these forms give deans to offer additional comments on such *positive* aspects of your record as honors, extracurricular activities, outside employment, and so on. Boston University's form makes the opportunity explicit: "If you are acquainted with the applicant and wish to add your evaluation of his or her ability, character, or motivation for law study, please do so."

Shrewd and forward-thinking applicants see this form as an opportunity to get to know their deans well before their senior year, or at least ask to sit down and talk with the dean face to face before he fills out the form. Creating a personal relationship that the dean can draw from may motivate him to provide value-added comments when your certification form hits his desk. The dean's certification offers you, in other words, an opportunity to transform a pro forma application checkmark into a full-fledged endorsement. Consider it a free recommendation waiting to be exploited.

APPROACHING RECOMMENDERS

Now that you know who you'd like to ask for recommendations, don't just fire off a few e-mails and wait for the effusive praise to pour in. A careful, proactive strategy toward approaching and coaching your recommenders can make all the difference between a disastrous "recommendation" and the real McCoy.

The first step is gauging whether your prospective recommenders are willing. In fact, you want them to be more than "willing"; you want them to be downright enthusiastic. The best method is to ask them forthrightly if they think they can write a strongly supportive letter. If you encounter anything short of unhesitating consent, you may want to consider someone else. Recommenders sometimes agree to write positive letters but then, in the spirit of objectivity (or worse), submit tepid or vague letters that harm more than they help. A recommender who is only writing a letter out of courtesy or duty will probably accept an opportunity to back out if you offer one. So phrase your request in language that invites the unenthusiastic recommender to recuse himself.

The Drill

Let's face it, devoting the multiple hours required to write a detailed letter of recommendation is a big favor. Give your recommenders enough time (two to three months is ideal), and make your initial request in a face-to-face meeting or two. Bring with you all the supporting documentation you think they need (or will read). Definitely give them:

- Your résumé and (if the recommender is a professor) your transcript: If you can customize separate résumés that emphasize different accomplishments for each recommender, so much the better.

- If the recommender is a professor, a list of the classes you've taken with the recommender, together with the grades you earned and one or two of your tests or papers from those classes: this is particularly important if you've been out of school for a while and need to jog the recommender's memory.

- Your schools' official recommendation letter form and stamped envelope; instructions for filling out the school's online form; or the recommender's letter, the LSAC's letter of recommendation form, and an envelope for sending them to LSAC—depending on which of these procedures your school prefers. Also provide recommenders with a list of your deadlines.

- A cover memo or general statement explaining why you want to go to law school, what your post-JD goals are, what you think is unique and compelling about your candidacy (traits, not just skills), why you selected them to write a recommendation, which examples (accomplishments) and themes you want this recommender to discuss, and which schools you're applying to, with a list of the qualities they seek in applicants.

Consider giving your recommenders:

- Your personal statement, if you've written it (you did start early, didn't you?) (note a risk here: the recommender may simply import material from your essay with no new insights or information)

- Talking points for addressing the topics that schools often suggest recommenders discuss in their recommendations, such as a summary of some of your greatest accomplishments under this recommender

- If the recommender is an employer, highlights and/or quotations from the recommender's performance reviews of you and perhaps some documentation related to your greatest success under this recommender

- A sample of a good letter of recommendation if you have one

- Accepted.com's "10 Tips for Recommenders" (at www.accepted.com/mba/LettersRec.aspx)

Be sure to tell your recommenders when you need the letter and how much time you realistically expect the process to take. Provided you don't overdo it, all this information can ensure that your recommendation letters complement your personal statement while minimizing the chances of a backfiring endorsement. Make clear that the recommender must respond with at least one specific and detailed example for each topic category that the school suggests the letter include. For example, Cornell's recommendation form hints: "We would appreciate your candid evaluation of this applicant's academic abilities and potential for success in the legal profession. Please include any information about the applicant's social or academic background or emotional makeup that we should consider, including character factors." We will discuss the most common topic categories later in this chapter.

Far from scripting the recommender's response, your supporting documentation may actually prod his or her memory about accomplishments and skills that you overlooked. In any event, your impressive organization and thoroughness is also likely to put recommenders in a frame of mind highly conducive to praise.

Educating Recommenders

If your recommender is a professor, he or she is likely to be a veteran of the recommendation letter game and thus may require little guidance. You must carefully judge, however, whether your recommender really understands the recommendation process. If he or she is young or in a discipline that sends few students to law school, or if you work for an organization whose employees rarely aspire to professional school, you may have to do some hand holding.

Similarly, your nonacademic recommenders may think they should approach your letter in the same spirit as your annual job reviews, using a tone of rigorously neutral objectivity. They may believe that an impersonal corporate tone confers weight and authority. Edify them: recommendation letters should start not from a position of neutrality but one of energetic advocacy.

Even if your nonacademic recommenders can't comment on your abilities in traditional law-related tasks like research and writing, have them comment on your performance in other situations that do resemble law school: putting in long hours, speaking before groups, reading reams of material, handling steep learning curves, functioning under enormous stress, and so on.

WRITING YOUR OWN?

More and more recommenders, weighed down by work and other responsibilities, are asking applicants to draft their recommendation letters for them. Even if your recommender only intends to use your draft as a starting point, you should resist this request for one good reason: law schools don't like it. The whole point of asking a third party—your favorite professor or boss—to provide some outside perspective on your potential and qualifications is defeated if that "outside" perspective comes directly from you.

Given that typical admissions officers read thousands of recommendation letters over their careers, you can believe they have a sixth sense about nongenuine letters. The personal idiosyncrasies of your writing and thinking style are difficult to hide, and after reading your personal statement, admissions officers are likely to be sensitive to them. Even if you try to adopt your recommender's voice, the similarity between your essays and your letters of recommendation is likely to be all too clear.

But the odds of getting caught are not the only argument against writing your own letters. Writing your own recommendation will probably produce a mediocre letter. You are unlikely to be able to view yourself or to handle language in the way that a more experienced individual will. Besides, even the most egotistical self-applicant will be hard put to describe himself with the same delighted, spontaneous enthusiasm that a truly supportive recommender can exude.

By writing your own letter, in other words, you'll be trading an opportunity to provide a fresh, deeper perspective on your candidacy for a warmed-over version of your personal statement and essays. So do your best to convince your recommender to write the letter him- or herself. If you can't, try to find another recommender who will. Needless—one hopes—to say, writing *and* signing the letter for the recommender (also known as forgery) is illegal and unethical.

If you really feel you have no choice but to write the letter for the recommender's signature, consider an alternative that will keep you out of the process. Accepted.com can interview your recommenders for you and transcribe their comments into formal recommendation letters for their revisions and signatures. This removes you from the process, as the schools want, and saves your recommenders from the hassle of slaving over nouns, predicates, and indirect objects. They may not have two hours to write your letter, but they are likely to have 30 minutes to convey their comments over the phone.

STRATEGIES FOR RECOMMENDATION TOPICS

Recommendation forms and instructions vary from school to school. Most law schools let recommenders decide what to write about, so long as the letter addresses the underlying question of your preparedness for law school and a law career. For this reason, most applicants only need to request a single basic letter from each of their recommenders, which can then be used for all their target schools. The use of such generic or one-size-fits-all recommendation letters has probably increased now that more law schools are requiring that applicants use the LSAC's Recommendation Letter Service, which includes a generic recommendation form.

However, the shrewd applicant will realize that what the LSAC's generic recommendation instructions ask for can differ significantly from the schools' recommendation forms, so a generic letter may not address everything a school wants discussed. The LSAC's instructions for recommenders read: "Law schools value your candid appraisal of the applicant's ability, academic and otherwise, to study law, including qualities of mind and character, dedication, responsibility, and readiness for the rigors of advanced academic study. Evidence of overcoming adversity, rising to challenges, and achieving beyond expectations is helpful in assessing candidates for admission." Nowhere does LSAC ask recommenders to comment about

- Your "maturity and judgment" or "concern for justice," which Boalt Hall invites recommenders to discuss

- Your "capacity for original and independent work," which Boston University wants to hear about

- Your "leadership in extracurricular, community, or work activity," which intrigues Columbia

- Your "special interests," which Harvard considers important

- Your "potential for success in the legal profession," which Cornell requires

Rather than hope that her recommenders' letters include enough useful information to satisfy all of her target schools, the shrewd applicant makes sure her recommenders comment on each of the topics that individual schools ask about. This may add to your recommender's burden and it may result in a longer letter than other applicants' submit, but it will ensure that each school learns what it wants to learn about you. These school-specific topic questions reflect each school's self-image, and you want to pay obeisance to that.

You can and should take this customization process one step further by asking recommenders who have specific experience with your target schools to mention that experience somewhere in the letter. They may have earned their JDs there, for example; hired or worked with people who did; or recommended successful applicants there previously. Or they may simply believe that a specific program the school offers is especially well suited for you. Always exploit opportunities to make your application school-specific.

Even customized, school-specific letters begin, however, with a core general letter. We'll discuss the essential topics for that letter next.

The General Recommendation Letter: Essential Topics

Survey the recommendation forms of U.S. law schools and you'll see a shared interest in the following basic topics:

- Duration and context of recommender's relationship with you

- Your intellectual, analytical, or scholarly skills

- Your writing, verbal, or communication skills

- Your character or personality

- Your weaknesses

We'll discuss each in turn, beginning with the letter's introduction.

Introduction

Recommendations have traditionally followed the format and conventions of the standard business letter. This means that some brief and general tone-setting language at the opening is appropriate: "It's my distinct pleasure to write this letter of recommendation on behalf of . . ." or "I'm delighted to have this opportunity to wholeheartedly endorse Joe Blow for admission to . . ." Such language establishes a note of enthusiasm that, ideally, will pervade the entire letter. The recommender can then follow with a summary of the theme of the letter—your distinctive qualifications for law school: "Svetlana's unusually analytical mind, love of research, and natural writing skills make her one of the most promising law school applicants I have encountered in 20 years of teaching."

If she feels inspired, your recommender could also open the letter a little more creatively with an anecdote about the first time you came to her office after class, the first time she saw the person behind your public persona, or a moment when you surprised her or outshone her expectations. This will not only immediately distinguish the letter from the stuffy norm, it will vividly demonstrate the recommender's special relationship with and regard for you. By engaging the reader's interest from the start, a personalized opening can also save your letter from the cursory yadda-yadda review that some recommendations receive (and usually deserve).

Above all, the introduction is an excellent place for the recommender to provide a few sentences of background information about herself: where she earned her degrees and which universities or organizations she has worked for and in what capacity. Such information enhances the recommender's credibility as someone who has the credentials to pass authoritative judgments on your intelligence and analytical skills, writing and verbal ability, and personal character. Recommenders who have law degrees should obviously note that fact, especially if they are alumni of the law school in question.

Finally, the opening paragraph can conclude with an explicit description of the pool of peers against which the recommender is comparing you, including the approximate number of people in that group: "all the law school applicants I've recommended in my career," "the 25 research assistants I've worked with in my research career," "the 50-odd paralegals our firm has employed," "the 30 summer interns the Agency has hired." The recommender then quantitatively ranks you within this group, for example, "upper 5 percent." This comparative-ranking statement, which can also be inserted at the end of the letter, is critically important, and the vast majority of schools specifically request it.

If your recommender is an academic, you can add significant value to this ranking statement by asking your recommender to compare you explicitly to previous law school applicants he or she has recommended. For example, "Sharena is easily the most talented of the 40 law school applicants I've recommended in my career." If your target school is a well-known law program or one that receives many applications from the recommender's school, the recommender may even add some powerful school-specific language: "Sharena is easily the most talented of the 15 applicants I've recommended to your school in my career." Or better still: "Sharena compares quite favorably to Ron Birkenstock, who earned his JD from your school last year, as well as to two of my other recent former students, who are now at Penn and UCLA Law."

If the law school has had good reason to value this recommender's evaluations—because his applicants have often been law review editors, for example—then these school-specific comparisons can be the most effective part of your recommendation. That's something to keep in mind both when you're choosing recommenders and when you're weighing whether to submit generic or customized recommendations.

How Long and in What Context?

Whether you're submitting a general letter through LSAC or a school-specific letter, your recommenders should take the trouble to establish that they know you well by specifically noting the range and depth of their interaction with you. Many recommenders falter here by omitting this context or dismissing it in a single sentence: "I've known Caldwell since October 2002, when he first took my graduate seminar on Poststructuralist Hermeneutics." Your recommender needs to go deeper than this and detail her relationship with you. What were the specific courses or work situations in which your recommender first came to know you? What were the difficulty levels of these courses and what was the recommender's grading policy? In what ways did you first stand out from the crowd, and what did you do to build a deeper relationship with the recommender than most others established? How often would you meet or talk with the recommender? How did the context or frequency of your interaction with the recommender change over time? How frequently do you interact with the recommender now, and in what sorts of circumstances? These are the sorts of detailed questions you need to address.

If this seems like overkill, remember that if your recommender can establish early on that she has extensive and sustained knowledge of you, she will have created a climate of credibility that will make all her upcoming assertions about you more believable. Conversely, if your relationship with the recommender is not particularly close or long-standing, you may want to keep this paragraph short and sweet—or consider another recommender.

Having established this detailed context as succinctly as possible, the recommender can conclude this section by explicitly asserting her authority to recommend you: "For these reasons, I believe I'm in a particularly strong position to comment authoritatively on Caldwell's skills and potential."

Academic, Intellectual, or Analytical Ability

For the vast majority of law students, the first year is a brutal experience. Under conditions of unremitting pressure and competitive intensity, you will be asked to begin thinking in a way you have never done before while absorbing and taking apart a staggering volume of reading material. That almost all law students survive this harrowing process is due in large part to the law schools' ability to select the people who've demonstrated the ability or potential to handle such intellectual tests in the past. Though they play a much less significant role in this process than do your LSAT scores and grades, recommenders can make (or break) your case for intellectual preparedness for law school. Their response to this topic is thus the most important part of the recommendation letter.

Luckily, academic ability can mean many different things, so you need not worry too much about demonstrating the capacity to "think like a lawyer." Law schools are interested in whether and how you dissect complex intellectual topics into logical parts and then manipulate these parts to reach some conclusion. But they're also interested in your general diligence as a student, your creativity or originality, and your intellectual standards and potential. These are broad enough categories to encompass almost any applicant's background.

If you are a liberal arts major, your recommender will focus on more qualitative and language-based types of intellectual activity than if you are a science major, for whom quantitative and empirical/inductive skills will be relevant. Quantitative abilities will also be the focus of recommenders who are writing for older applicants applying directly from the workforce. Employers will also be able to talk about the highly pragmatic, group-based intellectual skills that nonacademic environments require. Classroom papers and tests, lab work, research projects, formal theses, corporate analyses or reports, articles or projects for extracurricular organizations—all can demonstrate the kind of focused analytical intellectual ability that law schools seek.

The point is that your recommenders must make a substantial case, anchored by detailed examples, for your intellectual ability, but they need not worry too much about finding examples that fit the academic skills they imagine law schools will find relevant. The University of Virginia is the exception, not the rule, when it advises recommenders to discuss the applicant's "ability to read complex textual material closely, to analyze it carefully, and to present reasoned conclusions." Of course, if your recommender has examples that demonstrate this highly law school–relevant skill, all law schools will want to hear them, but the vast majority of schools do not explicitly expect the recommender to provide them.

Writing or Communication Skills

"Lawyers are professional writers." That fact, quoted from Emory Law School's instructions to applicants, is why almost every law school insists that recommenders discuss your verbal skills. You simply must be able to handle language confidently and express yourself well if you hope to succeed in law school and the law. Here again, schools will rely mainly on your personal statement for evidence that you can write, but recommenders' input can tip wavering scales one way or the other. If you are a liberal arts major and your recommender makes no mention whatever of your verbal skills (never mind subtly disparaging them), doubts may enter the adcom's mind that will add to the burden placed on your personal statement. Likewise, if you are an engineer and your recommender goes out of his way to provide examples of your unusual facility with the written and spoken word, you will have helped clear up a major adcom concern.

It doesn't matter what recommenders point to in establishing your communications skills. Term papers and theses, articles or speeches, class or corporate presentations before groups, language-teaching experiences, even the verbal dexterity you demonstrate in one-on-one meetings—all constitute excellent proof that you can walk the talk.

Character or Personality

Being educators, most recommenders will view evaluating your intellectual ability and writing skills as all in a day's work. After all, even if they don't remember you all that well, scanning your transcript and term papers will enable them to draw general conclusions about your academic skills. In contrast, only someone who has gotten to know you personally can persuasively discuss your character. Nothing exposes a superficial applicant–recommender relationship better than a character question. That's why the character or personality section of your recommendation is where you can be the most help to your recommender by suggesting appropriate stories to illustrate who you are.

In the narrowest sense, schools ask about your character because state bar examiners perform background checks on would-be attorneys to determine if they have the personal integrity to practice law. So, if your recommender can discuss your character by referring to specific examples of your integrity, she should do so. Perhaps she knows that you served on your college's honor code committee, she remembered the way you handled a classmate you saw plagiarizing, or she was impressed by your paper on "Notions of Personal Responsibility in Dostoevsky, Conrad, and Faulkner." If you are an older applicant, your recommender might relay an anecdote about the nuanced but ethically anchored way in which you handled a client's attempt to modify a report's findings or handled a difficult case of divided loyalties between supervisors.

Because integrity entails a clear sense of right and wrong and the ability to act on it, it can involve social ethics as well as personal ethics. That's why Columbia and Boalt Hall, respectively, invite recommenders to discuss your "concern for others" and "concern for justice." If your personal statement has a strong public interest theme, you will obviously want your recommenders to echo that theme strongly in their letters. For example, your academic recommender may have worked with you on a student club devoted to helping the community and your nonacademic recommender may have worked with you on the board of your local Red Cross. When UC Davis Law asks recommenders "Are you aware of the applicant's contribution to the college or community in non-academic endeavors?" it's really asking an integrity question: are you a selfless joiner and doer or a self-focused drone?

Character means much more than just integrity, of course. You'll see the word *maturity*, for example, on almost every law school's recommendation form. Schools want to know whether you are applying from deeply examined reasons or from lack of alternatives and whether you have what it takes to stick it out in law school. Here, encourage recommenders to cite examples of your contradicting the stereotype of the immature collegian by, for example, working full-time while in school, helping your family through a difficult period, serving as a resident assistant or student advisor, or completing a double major in four years while juggling leadership in varsity sports.

Maturity is one dividend of rising above obstacles, something that the LSAC recommendation form (as well as that of many individual schools) invites recommenders to discuss: "Evidence of overcoming adversity, rising to challenges, and achieving beyond expectations is helpful in assessing candidates for admission." If you have recommenders who know you as more than a face in a class or a name on an organization chart, you can encourage them to refer to ways in which you've successfully defeated obstacles, whether poverty, prejudice, or impairment.

The LSAC's form also gives prominent space to another critical aspect of character—uniqueness or diversity: "You may wish to include . . . how the candidate will add to the diversity of the law school." If you are an underrepresented minority, this is the place for your recommender to discuss how you have risen above the limitations others placed on you. But, as we saw in our discussion of diversity statements in chapter 3, law schools define diversity loosely as anything that makes you stand out from the crowd. Encourage your recommender to drive home your unique self-marketing handle by providing her with examples that can be used to show that you will enhance your law class's diversity, from your special interests to your unusual achievements and experiences.

Weaknesses

Though few law school recommendation forms specifically ask recommenders to comment on weaknesses, doing so can actually strengthen your application. Schools expect your recommenders to be quite supportive. Indeed, the flood of vaguely unsubstantiated praise they see every year breeds a natural skepticism. How refreshing, then, to encounter a recommender's frank admission that you aren't the first perfect human being. Even a brief weakness paragraph can go a long way toward overcoming the adcom's cynicism over yet another glowing recommendation letter. By providing contrast, weaknesses can, if they're not deal-breakers, actually accentuate your positives.

What weaknesses are acceptable? It's often a question of degree. A weakness—"poor communication skills"—that will expedite your file to the ding bin becomes tolerable if it's a mild, narrow, or correctable form of the flaw: "needs to polish her oral presentation skills." Such repairable weaknesses can include anything from "needs to be more thorough in scholarly research work" or "has a tendency toward linear thinking" to "too quick to compromise" or "immature about organizational politics." If, like these, your personal weakness is not egregious, doesn't routinely impede your effectiveness, and can be rectified, then admitting it may not damage your chances of admission. Avoid, however, the stale trick of dressing up virtues as vices: "perfectionist," "works too hard," "sometimes impatient with those who have lower standards." These have been trotted out by thousands of applicants since the dawn of time and will only prompt an eye-rolling yawn from weary adcoms.

Citing one weakness is sufficient, but a two-sentence response usually won't cut it. To make it credible, the recommender should be specific about the context or impact of the weakness and should indicate what you have been doing to rectify the flaw, including, ideally, a recent example of the new and improving you.

Once your recommender has identified one of your changeable weaknesses, the adcoms are in a position to believe her if she decides to help you do damage control on your *nonchangeable* weaknesses, like low LSATs or GPAs. The claim that your standardized test scores are not predictive is much more persuasive coming from a professor than from you.

Conclusion

Like the introductory paragraph, the conclusion sums up the main themes that distinguish you and, with a ringing final endorsement, completes the sustained tone of enthusiasm that should characterize the letter. If the recommender has not ranked you against your peers, he can do so here. Unless you're using a general "all-in-one" recommendation letter, the name of the target school can be repeated here to emphasize that the letter is tailored to the school.

If the law school's recommendation form doesn't ask the recommender to comment on your post-JD goals, you might encourage him to discuss them anyway in the conclusion, especially if you are an older applicant who, after all, is expected to have a clear idea why you need a JD. The greater the detail the recommender provides about your post–law school goals, the more thoughtful and forward-looking you will appear to be. For example, the recommender could explain why she believes you want a JD, why these goals are reasonable for you, and how the target school can help you achieve them. This section can be particularly effective if the recommender herself has a JD—ideally (but not necessarily) from the school in question.

It's usually also a good idea to have the recommender close the letter by sharing his or her direct phone number with the committee: "Please don't hesitate to call at (123) 456-7890 if you have any questions whatsoever about Nigel." This further demonstrates the recommender's enthusiasm by showing that he is willing to say even more. (It also reassures adcoms that the letter is legitimate, since no forger would invite the committee to uncover his deception.)

The Meat of the Letter: Examples

"General propositions do not make concrete cases." Surprisingly, Justice Oliver Wendell Holmes's sage counsel is not followed by the majority of recommenders. They dole out effusive praise in generous heaps, but, in the absence of specific supporting examples, the adcom is left to take the recommenders on their word. It's because of this that schools' recommendation forms plead for credible evidence:

- "Please include reference to any specific events, impressive accomplishments, or unusual circumstances that may give us added insight." [George Mason]

- "It would be most helpful if you would cite specific facts upon which your appraisal is based." [Boston University]

- "Letters that are relatively specific and detailed tend to be the most useful." [Boalt Hall]

As with essays, the most persuasive evidence is the example or anecdote. After making a general assertion about you in a theme sentence or two—"One of Glenda's special talents is thorough research."—the body of the paragraph (several sentences in length) consists of evidence sentences that cite specific examples of your strength. "I was quite impressed when Glenda supplemented her research of the key secondary sources by requesting and gaining permission to examine

Stephen Douglas's personal papers at the University of Illinois." These kinds of "for example" statements are the payload, the life blood, of the recommendation letter—proof that your recommender isn't just blowing laudatory smoke rings. Without them, your letter becomes instantly forgettable.

As in essays, such mini-accomplishments can usually be broken down into three parts:

1. What was the problem or challenge that you faced? (For example, "Writing a senior thesis that proves that Douglas should have won the 1860 election.")

2. What specifically did you do to analyze and then solve the problem? What was unusual or impressive about the solution you found? (For example, "not only reviewed key secondary sources but primary sources as well. Showed that Douglas himself believed that two tactical blunders cost him the election.")

3. What was the impact or end result for you and/or the organization of solving the initial problem? (For example, "won departmental honors for senior thesis.")

If your recommender's examples can be backed up by quantitative evidence (for example, if you're a nontraditional applicant working for a business), encourage him to do so. Numbers give adcoms hard data they can hang their hats on, magically transforming the nebulous into the tangible. If your recommenders back up their claims about you with concrete numbers, your letters will gain weight and credibility.

Make sure that your recommender's examples don't exactly match the ones you use in your personal statement. One of the functions of a recommendation letter is to provide new information, and you don't want to create the impression that you have a limited number of impressive stories. As a rule of thumb, for every three examples or anecdotes that your recommender refers to, two should be unique to the recommendation and one a story you also discussed in your essays.

Finally, it's not enough to provide stellar examples if you don't also provide the context for understanding them. Your recommender shouldn't just state that you performed all the research for the middle three chapters of her monograph, for example. She should explain that she's only given one other student that much responsibility in a quarter century of teaching—and he just made law review at the school you're applying to.

With your personal statement, essays, and letters of recommendation fleshed out, polished, and submitted you've done all you can to ensure that your all-important numbers are viewed in the best context. If you've followed the advice in this book, you will have done more than the vast majority of applicants do—taken complete control of your law school application. Your fate is now in the hands of the gods, but, whatever the result, you can take comfort in knowing you've done the best you possibly can.

Sample Documents

PERSONAL STATEMENT OUTLINE

Sample 1

Accepted at University of Florida Levin College of Law, Florida State University, and Florida Coastal School of Law

    I. Hook to grab reader and introductory paragraph
      A. "Ouch!" Describe briefly how, two years ago, a dentist hit a nerve drilling while giving me an unnecessary root canal.
      B. While this image may make some think of Laurence Olivier as Josef Mengele drilling into the mouth of Dustin Hoffman in the movie "Marathon Man," it has helped crystallize thoughts about becoming a lawyer.
      C. Briefly note that I have been building a case over the last two years through the Board of Health that was just decided by the Board of Dentistry.
   II. Highlights of pre-college education
      A. After several moves, family settled in the Ft. Lauderdale area.
      B. Life carried along somewhat as expected for a young teenager.
         1. Played football for my middle school.
         2. To improve the quality of my education, parents sent me to a Catholic school for high school. Smaller. College prep.
         3. Downside, I was no longer qualified for the school's football team—St. Thomas managed to have one of the best football teams in the state because it imported stars, giving them scholarships.

    4. Satisfied my love of sports by playing in city basketball and soccer leagues.

    5. Worked three times a week at a pizza restaurant. Hard work but what can be wrong with getting enough tips to pay my car insurance.

  C. Academically, I was good in math and science but concentrated on economics, government, and history.

  D. One truly enjoyable course proved to be pivotal.

    1. Describe Mr. Williams' economics course.

    2. What I did and enjoyed.

    3. How my team prospered.

III. College

  A. Entering as an engineering student, on a Florida Bright Futures Scholarship.

  B. Soon switched to being a business major, concentrating on finance.

    1. U of F had a good business school.

    2. Wanted to renew the excitement I experienced in Mr. Williams' course, when I even started investing my own money and enjoyed reading books on business, markets, finance.

    3. Now, I am particularly enjoying the active involvement possible in my upper-level courses.

      a. Explain how lower-level courses are taught via TV.

      b. Note my appreciation for a more dynamic, interactive approach. (This is more similar to law school.)

      c. Equity market course—doing quite well.

      d. Dean's List.

  C. Became active in my fraternity.

    1. Obviously for social reasons. Have enjoyed traveling to college games and on vacations with my fraternity friends, etc.

    2. Gained significant experience and confidence from:

      a. Being officer and managing budget and employees.

      b. Elected member of the standards board—chosen because people think I am fair and open-minded.

      c. Efforts with the Surf Rider Foundation—explain.

  D. Family has remained important to me.

    1. Enjoyed the 12-day cruise through Europe.

      a. Italy, Spain, Greece, France, Turkey.

      b. Especially loved seeing Pompeii. Describe what intrigued me.

    2. As undergraduate years drawing to an end and I began thinking about my own desire to have a career, family, etc., began wondering if becoming a lawyer would gratify me.

    3. Then, the dentist jabbed me!

  E. Last summer, tested out this idea by arranging a summer internship with Hendelman & Muskat P.A. Law Firm—a real estate firm.

1. Describe experiences in closings, what I contributed.
2. Describe my particular interest in contracts.
3. The experiment was a success—I confirmed that I would enjoy the day-to-day work of being a lawyer.

IV. Becoming a lawyer
   A. At this point, I am inclined to become a real estate lawyer or remain in some business-related law.
   B. However, I am currently exploring the Judge Advocate General's Corp as a possibility after law school.
      1. Attractive because of the variety of options.
      2. Possibility of handling cases right out of school.
   C. XXX law school is particularly attractive to me because its xxx provides a good match with my skills, interests, and goals.

V. Conclusion—With the skills I will gain at XXX law school and the responsible fair-mindedness that I am known for, I am confident that I will be a lawyer that people respond to with a well-meant "thank you" and not an "ouch!"

PERSONAL STATEMENTS

Sample 2

Accepted at University of Memphis Humphreys School of Law, University of Miami School of Law, St. Thomas University School of Law, South Texas College of Law, Thomas Jefferson School of Law, Golden Gate University School of Law, and Georgia State University College of Law

Bundling up to protect myself from the cool morning breeze, I stood with my six new friends, eagerly awaiting the first glimpse of the morning sun. I've seen many sunrises in my life, but this one was different. I attributed the nervous energy flowing through me to the electrifying history of the ground I walked on. My friends and I were standing on top of Masada in southern Israel, a great mountain with even greater symbolic importance to the history of Israel and its people. Trying as hard as I could to absorb every second of this magical event, I then realized what made it so surreal: of the seven people standing in our group, I was the only one who knew everyone else—I was the common link that had brought this group of teens together. Then I realized how often this same thing happens in my life—I have an innate ability to bring people together, especially people from different social groups who might not otherwise meet. Perhaps because this realization occurred at such a magical place, I decided that day that I would find a career where I could combine this ability and my passions to help other people.

It happens all the time. A friend will call asking me if I know someone in another city for whatever reason. When I do (which is quite often) I give them a phone number or email address for that person and the contact is made. I am a common link for many people. Recently, my friend Alicia was stuck in the Phoenix airport with an eight-hour delay and called me to see if I knew anyone who could help her. As a matter of fact, I did, gave Alicia my friend's phone number, and the two met and went out for dinner and a drink! As another example, during my internship at Universal Studios' corporate office, a colleague, a filmmaker, asked me if I knew anyone involved with the New England Film Festival in Burlington, Vermont, who might help him get his film presented. As a matter of fact, I did, and, sure enough, the following spring my colleague was in Burlington showing his movie at the festival. I often view creating these connections as a puzzle or a game: how can I advance this person's problem, question, or idea through the vast network of acquaintances I've accumulated for the past twenty-two years? There's always an answer.

Once I realized that I had this gift, the question has always been what best to do with it? Aside from my family, two things drive my interest more than any others: music and helping my community. When I am not helping people I am reading about, listening to, or seeing a musical performance. Many people go to concerts to hear a song or some music they like; I go to truly experience the music. I immerse myself in the notes being played as if they are the last sounds I will ever hear. Last summer, this passion inspired me to organize a three-week group venture from San Diego up the Pacific Coast to Vancouver. Along the way, my friends and I would see my favorite band play eight different concerts, culminating in a two-day festival in Vancouver. This was going to be the vacation of a lifetime, but I needed parental approval first. So I prepared an exhaustive formal presentation that anticipated every objection, complete with maps, notes, dates, and a list of reasons. After my parents agreed, I then planned the entire trip for our 13-member group, from renting an RV for the 1,300-mile trip to making hotel reservations and lining up tickets. There is nothing I won't do for music.

Helping my community is my other passion, and I have long sought out activities and jobs that enable me to do just that. Working at a day camp during my summers enabled me to teach children while ensuring they had fun, and volunteering at places like the Burlington Halfway House or Senior Aid while at the University of Vermont enabled me to cook for and serve dinner for people less privileged than myself. As much as I enjoyed these activities, when I discovered an opportunity to combine my two great passions, I jumped at it. As a member of "Rock and Wrap It Up," I got to go backstage at major concerts, gather the leftover catered food, and then deliver it to a local homeless shelter or food bank. Working with such concerts as Crosby, Stills, Nash, and Young, Bob Dylan, and the Dave Matthews Band, I was able to meet many of the artists, and proud to tell them what I was doing for my community.

But what career would enable me to combine my ability to organize and connect diverse people with my passions for music and helping my community? The first time I contemplated a law career I was a sixth-grader spellbound by the movie "Twelve Angry Men." I particularly enjoyed the process of solving the case and the amount of energy the jurors put into solving it. Throughout my junior high and high school years I fueled my curiosity with a string of Grisham novels. Then in my third year at the University of Vermont, I took a Legal Environment in Business class that gave me a broad, objective vision of the law. To this day, that class remains one of the most interesting and memorable courses I've ever taken. Finally, conversations with Mr. Timmerman, attorney for my employer, Markham Talent Management, cemented my decision to pursue a career in law.

Though I remain open to the discoveries I will make in law school, my goal is to pursue a career in entertainment law or contract law, where I can use my knowledge to enlist and represent a group of entertainment/media industry clients as their agent, preparing and negotiating contracts and defending the interests of a diverse range of entertainers and musicians. Over the last four years I have taken classes to prepare myself academically for this future, including courses in persuasion, communication, and negotiation. My involvement in such extracurricular organizations as the University of Vermont's Sports Entertainment and Marketing Association has also honed my knowledge of the entertainment industry and its issues, from actor's contracts to copyrights.

"Love what you do, and do what you love" has always been my father's advice when it comes to careers. I know that a law degree is the best way to bring together my skill for connecting people and my passions for music and community service. I know that not everyone has the chance to have a career that they enjoy and are passionate about so I will embrace the opportunity the Thomas Jefferson School of Law offers with dedication and energy. As I said, I'm a connector. I've kept in touch with those six friends I met on Masada, and I made a deal with the two who are also planning to attend law school: when we all earn our J.D.'s we will return to Israel and meet one morning on Masada again. I'm sure we'll all have grown in many different ways.

Sample 3

Accepted at Lewis & Clark College Northwestern School of Law

My family lived through most of the Gulf War in the Qasr Air Force Base in Kuwait. But when the bombs started falling closer and closer to the base, I left with my mother and two younger brothers for Qatar. My father, an air force general, remained on the base; and I—the oldest male in a traditional Arab family—suddenly became the head of our family. Fortunately, he had already instilled in me a powerful sense of responsibility. What he left for me to discover, however, was the thing that I was passionate about.

When life returned to some state of normality, I finished high school with the top grade of "Excellent." Shell Oil offered me a full scholarship in the United States. I saw it as a great opportunity to meet new people, explore different cultures, and introduce my own culture to others. While my interest in chemistry continued in college, I decided to minor in business administration. In Kuwait, I had started a small business with my brother that specialized in high-end performance car parts and wheels. As a student in the United States, I expanded the business—an effort requiring about ten hours a week of my time and providing me with terrific experience in negotiating prices and exposure to different tariff laws.

During the summer of my sophomore year, I became engaged the traditional Arabic way—my family arranged the match. Shortly after the "contract writing" ceremony, however, it became evident that the contract was not to be fulfilled. This is not an easy situation in Muslim life, more tantamount to a divorce than simply a broken engagement. The legal and familial issues dragged on for a full year and my life suffered from it. It was not until my senior year that my grades rebounded. By then, I was also guardian of my younger brother, who had come to the United States.

By this time, I was also aware that chemical engineering alone was not going to be the exciting career I had hoped for. Luckily, Shell made an auspicious request of me. Expressing a need for lawyers with engineering backgrounds, they asked me to attend a seven-day course given by the National Institute of Legal Education (NILE). The very first day thrilled me. The professor rushed into the lecture room and started drilling us with questions. His powerful presence, as he talked and walked around the room catching everyone's attention, inspired me. Another professor presented the following dilemma: A car falls off a bridge and hits a tanker that explodes causing a large construction crane to fall on an aquarium. The windows of the aquarium shatter releasing sharks that bite two young girls who are disabled for life. "Who is responsible? Who do you sue?" he demanded of us. Such cases were intellectually challenging. Like chemical engineering, it required an analytic mind. "Analyze, take apart, see how every piece works." But in addition, there was the emotional element, the human factor I had missed in engineering alone.

When I returned to Kuwait, I reported to my job as a process engineer in a sulfur plant of one of the world's largest oil refineries. Soon, I was responsible for the process and mechanical aspects of the plant. Currently, I am a plant engineer in the Natural Gas Liquids Division. I work with people from all over the world— a challenge that requires good communication and interpersonal skills.

One day at the plant particularly sticks out: It was just before closing time; a scream came through all the radios in the refinery. "Disaster . . . Disaster . . . Shutdown . . . We have a fire!" I remained calm, although I realized that an explosion caused by the high operating pressures and temperatures in the plant issuing the distress call could create severe damage within a fifty mile radius. I immediately headed to the disaster control center to assist in handling the situation. There, I found a friend of mine, who was dying from the burns he had suffered. As I held him, words from the NILE course became painfully real: "Who was responsible? Who do you sue?" It was no longer simply an academic exercise when I was asked to prepare a report that was to be used in the legal action against the contractor who built the plant. I understood the importance of our laws and legal system in my heart.

I have found my passion and my responsibility. My passing knowledge of the law is no longer sufficient for me to accomplish what I want to do. My short-term goal, after I finish studying, is to serve Shell in the legal issues that arise every day in the oil business. In the longer term, when the time is right and I have gained enough experience, I hope to establish my own legal and engineering consulting business. Attending the Northwestern School of Law of Lewis and Clark will best serve my goals. The Business and Commercial Law program is of particular interest to me. Another great advantage is the school's specialization in Environmental and Natural Resources Law. I also find the school's exceptionally low student to faculty ratio very attractive. Conversely, I hope that my cultural, educational, and professional backgrounds will add much to the diversity of your school.

My father taught me how to be responsible and how to take charge. Once I thought I could do this simply with my mind and that being a chemical engineer would suffice. Now I know I have to do it also with my heart. I am counting the days until I can again experience the excitement of studying law and looking forward to the time when I can command the same presence as that professor who so challenged me on the first day of the NILE course.

Sample 4

Accepted at Golden Gate University School of Law

Our team of four women had raced sailboats together as teammates and competitors many times over the years. We became good friends and were delighted at the invitation to represent the United States in the Women's World Championships in Italy. Traveling separately from our different home states, we joined together in Portofino, Italy and spent the next several days preparing to work together mentally and physically, as well as learning about prevailing wind, wave, and tidal conditions. In addition to getting a clear start and maintaining good boat speed, our strategy was to play a winning tactical game on the course.

After six days of windy racing, our team won the regatta. It was the United States in first, Netherlands in second, and Germany in third. The reason for our success? We consistently worked together in *all* of the races that made up the regatta. It's not winning each individual race but consistently placing among the top finishers of each race that makes the scores' average an overall win. An average score of big wins and big losses generally loses the regatta. We had to pick and choose our risks and ensure each race counted toward the final win. Winning sailboat races requires three basics: a well-tuned boat, excellent teamwork, and a thorough understanding of the rules and courses. Each crewmember must trust the capabilities of the other members. The positions are clearly defined for each member, yet each must adjust to new roles as dynamics arise during a race. Success in sailing, as in life, requires seizing opportunities as well as practicing the four P's: planning, preparation, passion and patience.

I have been fortunate to win the Women's World championships in sailing in Newport, RI in 1987 and in Portofino, Italy in 1992. In 1988 and 2000, the St. Francis Yacht Club in San Francisco recognized me as an outstanding sailor who represented the club in furthering the sport and the integrity of sailing. The grandest awards of all, though, have been the lessons I've learned about teamwork and preparation, the philosophy I've absorbed, and the extraordinary people I've met along the way.

For many years I have raced with an Olympic Silver medalist in yachting who is also a lawyer. He taught me how to approach the racing rules to gain a competitive advantage. The trick is to understand and articulate the rules better than your competitors, both on the water and in a post-race protest hearing. A protest committee, similar to a qualified jury, generally hears a protest during a race at the end of the day. In order to win a protest, you must be able to present the facts clearly and concisely in a casual manner within the rules. I am proud of both my ability to do this and of how I readied myself for law school by living according to sailing's four P's.

I am the second daughter of four children born in Rhodesia, Africa to an English father and a Dutch mother. While managing a copper mine in Africa, my father pursued mining engineering work and accepted a position in California in 1965. When I was six, I became a first generation immigrant processed though the well-known gates of Ellis Island. Though my parents divorced when I was 12, my public high school days in Santa Barbara were happy. I did, however, grow up during an odd contradiction in society's thinking concerning women. I was not expected to marry and have children, but neither was I encouraged to have a professional career. Through my own decision and motivation, I pursued college. I majored in biology because I was fascinated by how cells develop and grow, how the immune system thrives and weakens, and the role of organic chemistry. I supported my college education through work, grants, scholarships, and loans.

Just as I was completing college, the personal computer era took flight. Though I did all of my college papers on a typewriter, I did have access to the University of California's mainframe computers for calculations and programming classes. I learned BASIC programming from a required course. I didn't realize at the time that skill would lead me to my first real job as a BASIC programmer for a company that made LORAN C navigation equipment. My job was to take the raw input data such as wind speed and direction, compass headings, and boat speed from the boat's instruments. I would compare the data to predict boat speeds under optimal conditions and display the variance between the two sets of data on an onboard computer. If the boat was not up to optimal speed, we could make sail trim or rig tune adjustments to increase the speed. I worked on this project my last year of college and my first year out of school.

In a career move, I took on marketing and technical sales for the communication division of Motorola. Initially our products revolved around two-way radio infrastructures, radios and pagers. We then rode the cellular technology wave as the leader of that industry. We built the infrastructures, marketed the concept, and sold the phones. Ten years later, in 1992, I began to explore other career horizons. Two areas of continued education intrigued me—law and business. I took both the LSAT and the GMAT. My first choice was to study technology law. I had to work during the day, however, and I did not think a part-time evening program would be the best approach to getting a law degree. I chose business school, taking a class or two at a time and working during the days. The schedule was demanding but exciting. I entered business school just as business philosophy was changing from re-engineering business processes to e-business solutions and electronic process solutions. I was very aware of the shift in business trends in the mid to late 1990's.

In 1995, I moved to Malibu, California and transferred from the graduate program at University of San Francisco to Loyola Marymount University in Los Angeles. As I continued with school, I briefly put my work career on hold to do volunteer work for Meals-on-Wheels and raise three fabulous stepchildren.

I now have the experience, the drive, the verve, the financial ability, and the time to pursue law as a full time student. One of my volunteer partners with Meals-on-Wheels, Rick Cupp, is a full time Law professor at Pepperdine University. His encouragement has been very motivating to me. In his words, "The best student I have ever had is a practicing civil attorney who graduated at 46 from Pepperdine. She brought wisdom to the discussions. Diversity in age is invaluable to the field of law." My focus will be family law. I believe my education, wisdom and competitive spirit are an excellent blend for success and that through law, I can make a strong impact on the lives of people.

Just as I cherish the outstanding sailor awards given to me in 1988 and again in 2000 in recognition of excellence and perseverance, I will cherish my law degree in 2004, truly knowing the planning, preparation, passion and patience with which I reached my goal and with which I'll practice.

Sample 5

Accepted at Rutgers University School of Law at Newark

When I saw him with the ax, I thought my life would flash before my eyes, with images of family vacations, holidays and other happy events. He was an angry twelve-year-old boy in foster care and I was the wicked Case Manager who had just told him he had to go to summer school. Instead of the flash, I got stuck on the question of how I ended up in this small west Texas town, with a crazed pre-teen, who seriously wanted me dead, when growing up, I wanted to become a cruise director on a luxury ship that sailed to exotic islands!

The answer to that question is simple. Cruise director's jobs were not readily available to a young college graduate, so, when I read an ad in the Austin paper that read "work with troubled children and youth," I answered the ad. After all, I had been a camp counselor and a life guard and those kids were lots of trouble. I got the job, still unsure about what a foster child was! While I seemed to have started my career on a fluke, my decision to become a child advocacy lawyer is about as premeditated as can be.

Obviously, I survived this early episode working in foster care. I seemed to have been a natural. The child screamed, "I'm not going to no g** d*** m***** f***** summer school and you can't make me," and I heard my mother's calm, firm voice come out of my mouth, "the name of the school is not g** d*** m***** f***** summer school, it is Travis Elementary. Now, put the ax back in the barn, I'm going inside. When you find your good feelings, we will discuss it." Then, I turned around and slowly began walking toward the house, praying he would not come running up behind me. When I glanced back, he was walking, head bent down, dragging the ax on the ground behind him. The foster mother yelled from the kitchen, "So how did he take the news." A smile came across my face, "Well, he didn't kill me."

That was thirteen years ago and I have stayed committed to this field, even working full-time time while I earned a Masters Degree in Educational Psychology from the University of Houston. As my career advanced from direct-care positions into increasingly responsible administrative ones, I was regularly exposed to the legal system and its impact on the lives of children in foster care. Periodically, I contemplated going to law school, but I felt I still had a lot more I could learn and accomplish doing what I was doing. It was only within the last few years that I began to feel that I had reached a ceiling in both my job satisfaction and my potential to make a real impact on children's lives.

Recently, I was invited by the Texas Department of Protective and Regulatory Services to sit on the committees that were rewriting the policies of the foster care system to conform to new state legislation—work I found extremely exciting. As a participant in this process, however, I realized how the good-will of the lawyers and law-makers was thwarted because of their lack of direct experience in the system. But I was a witness regularly to how the changes in both state and federal regulations caused children to be adopted or returned to their families before they were ready; inevitably, they were back in foster care within a few months. My experience on these committees has led to my decision to become a child advocacy lawyer, a profession in which I can achieve greater effectiveness on issues I care deeply about—the personal bonus is that I look forward again to greater job satisfaction.

The X Law School's program in child advocacy particularly attracts me because . . . *[School-specific info here]*

In return, I feel I will be an asset to the program. My work with abused and neglected children and their families is significant to understand the implications of the legal statutes and decisions that affect the lives of a traumatized population. My maturity and knowledge can be beneficial to younger students who may not fully grasp the nature of the work they are considering. I can also be a peer support for those students who have a difficult time dealing with the abusive situations their clients experienced.

As a lawyer, I will continue my role as an advocate for abused and neglected children, a role, as it turns out, I am a natural at.

Sample 6

Accepted at Whittier College Law School

My uncle and I have always been close. When I was a child, we spent hours together rebuilding engines, competing to catch the largest fish from Lake Champlain, and learning how to snowboard together in Alpine Valley. It was consequently shocking, as well as disappointing, that he waited two years to tell me that he had been diagnosed with Retinitis Pigmentosa (RP), an inherited eye disease that affects the photoreceptor cells in the retina. There is no cure for RP, and though its progress differs among individuals, its end result is always blindness.

My uncle's case started mildly, but his vision has become progressively worse over the years. Today he can see only the largest of objects faintly, has trouble walking, and is unable to drive. Witnessing how my uncle's condition has compromised his ability to take part in the activities we enjoyed so much made me realize how much I have taken my own health for granted. Prompted by both this realization and my uncle's affliction, I began volunteering at the American Braille Academy, a nonprofit organization that provides services for the visually impaired. To some, the individual tasks I performed—stocking books in the library, reading aloud, and helping people to learn life skills—may seem trivial. Such tasks, however, are offered to assist disabled individuals cope with their disability, including setting long term goals for their lives. These goals are invariably no different than those of any other person: to live an independent life engaged in fulfilling work and connected to loved ones.

However, my work at the Institute has made me realize that such objectives are often very difficult for disabled individuals to achieve. For example, I met a woman at the Institute who, like my uncle, was recently diagnosed with RP. After thirty years of working for an accounting firm, Helene was fired because she needed additional time to complete her tasks. Such cases of discrimination extend beyond employment to affect almost *every* aspect of a disabled person's life, from accessing public buildings to procuring housing and medical insurance. Although laws such as the Americans with Disabilities Act and Fair Housing Amendment exist, they are often not enforced because individuals lack either the knowledge or the ability to pursue their rights. In the case of Helene, she elected not to pursue legal action because she couldn't afford it.

My desire to attend law school is rooted in the recognition that individuals with disabilities require advocacy to realize their rights. Barriers such as discrimination or ignorance of the law often require legal intervention to obviate. I believe that with the right support system, individuals with disabilities can become successful, independent contributors in our society. My goal as an attorney is to facilitate this process and ensure that disabilities such as blindness do not prevent a person from achieving an independent, fulfilling life.

Working for American Braille Academy taught me a great deal about people with life altering disabilities, but it was not until I unexpectedly ran into my uncle there that it truly hit home. Previously, we had not talked too extensively about his condition, and it was an awkward moment for both of us. After speaking with him, however, I understood his reluctance to tell me about his condition, and that his reticence to see me afterward stemmed from his fear of losing his independence. With organizations like American Braille Academy operating in conjunction with the enforcement of the laws that guarantee rights, this doesn't have to be the case. My uncle and I are now close friends again. His ability to learn and adapt to his condition has inspired me to cope with the obstacles I face in my own life, and has strengthened my resolve to help him and others like him live the fulfilling lives they deserve.

Sample 7

Accepted at University of Houston Law Center and Arizona State University College of Law

I never would have imagined that arguing in favor of corporal punishment would lead me to law school. As a high school senior in varsity debate, my task was to create an affirmative case on the topic of increasing academic achievement in secondary schools in the United States. Finding evidence to establish a problem in the status quo was not the issue. The challenge was to produce a solution that could withstand strict rebuttal. After reading an article supporting the effectiveness of corporal punishment in early education, I decided to create a solid argument on this issue. Accordingly, I searched for more information that supported the positive effects of corporal punishment on learning. After finding enough evidence to present this case, I set up a debate that nobody expected to hear. I placed third in my first varsity competition, but more importantly, I enjoyed arguing about this controversial issue so much that my success affirmed my creative tendencies, and spawned the idea of going to law school.

While my debate experience encouraged me to explore all sides of a situation, I also realized that I enjoyed investigating new approaches to situations when I began to play guitar and learn about music promotion. Using the family computer, I wrote one-track compositions and explored different musical effects. After two years of experimenting, I recorded my first multi-track demo, "All for Now." This flute and synthesizer instrumental won first place for Denver artists on MP3.com in the early weeks of its release. I had found an outlet where I could expand on my originality, looking outside traditional thought and independently creating abstract musical arrangements. Since then, I have added to my collection of recording equipment and am currently in the process of crafting my first full-length album.

Much as I sought a different way to debate, and an opportunity to compose and produce music, I found myself trying to find new ways to learn class material throughout college. During a course in management and informational systems, my professor thought I had a talent for interacting with large groups of people. She suggested that I develop this potential by accepting a coveted position as a student assistant for her classroom at the beginning of the next semester. This position required interaction with over a thousand students, whom I was asked to help prepare for exams and the course finale—the University of Colorado Business Fair. As the professor expected, students were quick to pursue my assistance. I had one group of students who needed help building the mandatory "business fair booth," for which the groups were only given four by four foot areas. Since their product was a unique showerhead, I suggested that they first construct a very small bathroom to follow a theme, but also to do what others had neglected—to build *up* since they could not build out of the 4-foot area. Since appearance was a key element to having one's product noticed, building a second floor not only gave them more room to display their work, but attracted more attention to their booth.

Based on my performance in this position and my academic credentials, the University of Colorado Department of Economics asked me to work as a paid supplemental instructor for a microeconomic principles course, attending the professor's lecture each day, and then teaching two independent reviews. My task was to reinforce the information taught in class, challenge students to think critically, and foster independent results. On my first day, I entered the room with a pocket full of chalk, ready to give a full-on lecture. I glanced over the classroom and began to speak, covering textbook material. As soon as the chalk hit the board, I knew something was wrong. I paused and pondered the situation, recognizing that the silence was deafening. My misconception was to follow the format that previous instructors had used, simply restating the classroom material in lecture. Alternatively, I walked towards the class and helped the students push their desks together. After allowing a few moments for the students to introduce themselves, I explained that this would not be a class of dry lecture, but a stage to learn classroom material by real world problem solving and exploring ideas by interacting with peers. Rather than simply "teach," I finished the year by leading the class through their exercises, offering individual assistance when necessary. Ultimately, I had a successful teaching semester, with student-teacher evaluations and grades showing a strong positive correlation between my supplemental instruction sessions and classroom performance.

With this background of debating, developing new approaches, and learning communication skills, the study of law seems natural. As an attorney, I will interpret an issue and reflect on it abstractly, critically, and creatively much as I would when teaching microeconomic principles or creating a new song. Furthermore, I will use the practical ideas of business and apply them to my role as a lawyer. Specifically, I will have the chance to pursue a developing interest in tax law, an area of study closely related to my interest in economics. Eventually, I plan to take the knowledge that I develop throughout my career and go back to teaching. Although I feel confident that I will never again be arguing the merits of corporal punishment, I look forward to using my creative abilities to address legal issues from a unique and innovative point of view.

Sample 8

Accepted at Southwestern University School of Law

There I sat, ten years old, in a tube of metal running at 70mph under the great expanse of New York City. Only one month before, I was walking along the seawall in Georgetown, Guyana, the small South American country where I was born. My great-grandparents had migrated to this part of the West Indies island chain from India during the period of British Imperialism. They began working on the vast English-owned sugar estates. By the time I was born, much had changed but Guyana remained vastly different from America. For example, in Guyana there were more homes without indoor plumbing than with plumbing. Children played in the streets with hundreds of other neighborhood kids, inventing games using whatever they found. Until the day that I moved to the United States in 1987, I had never seen a television. Sitting on that subway, realizing how little I knew of the American way of life, I was overwhelmed by fear—of the unknown, of having to start over from scratch, of not fitting into my new environment.

Now, sixteen years later, I cherish what I have been able to accomplish and the way that the stark contrast in lifestyles provided me with important lessons about maintaining the motivation to succeed despite having to adapt to new cultures and the value of maintaining a strong sense of community. With persistence and the support of family and community, I have completed an undergraduate degree in Business Administration from California State University Northridge and a Master's Degree in Business Administration at California State University Northridge. I have also enjoyed four years of increasing responsibility in corporate positions, ending as a Sales Analyst reporting directly to the VP of Sales at Earthlink Network. I have gained exposure to cutting edge technologies, the Internet boom and emerging legal issues. In the Buffalo Spammer case, Earthlink filed legal charges against an individual who allegedly stole the identities of some of their consumers. Later, in another case, Earthlink was involved in a suit concerning file sharing when the record industry started trying to hold ISPs responsible for their consumers who downloaded music. I observed the evolution of laws and governmental action in response to new technologies and wanted to rise higher in my career, perhaps especially because in Guyana, most women do not achieve higher education. The professions for women are limited to either teaching or housekeeping, and the choice usually depends upon a family's social level. There are no opportunities for women to get MBAs or to become lawyers. In America, where opportunities are available to everyone, I became highly motivated to take advantage of them and decided to pursue an MBA.

Because in Guyana, life is community oriented, I had tremendous support from my family, who always encouraged me to strive for the best when it comes to school and to work. My father is a teacher, and he has always instilled in me the importance of education. In addition to financial support, my family provided emotional support. When I was working through my graduate program, my dad sometimes cooked enough food for a week and stocked it in my fridge so I was able to have home-cooked food. That gesture meant a lot to me during stressful periods where I doubted I could complete my program. Since I have learned first-hand the benefits of a strong family environment, I offer support and encouragement to classmates and colleagues, creating the understanding that the best way to overcome obstacles is by working together.

In addition to establishing team spirit, I also know how to help others learn to organize themselves around their workload. Earning my Master's in Business Administration, which is one of my greatest accomplishments, I developed my capacity to prioritize and multi-task. I combined a full-time job with a full-time school schedule for two years, managing my time efficiently and effectively. Being a full-time student while holding a full-time work position also taught me how to carefully manage my personal tolerances for physical stress. To help maintain balance, I set aside a period of time everyday where I did something completely unrelated to work or school. Sometimes this would mean fifteen minutes for reading a fashion magazine or an hour to go to a yoga class. Another thing I learned to help maintain balance was keeping my focus on the task at hand. I learned to consciously focus on my work when I was at work and to block out everything else and then, similarly, when I was in class to focus on studies. This helped me to keep things organized and to not get overwhelmed. With this kind of balance in my life, I could push myself to accomplish whatever proved challenging.

As an undergraduate, I had never found my classes too difficult. However, that changed in the graduate program. Sitting in a lecture hall of over 60 people in my first CSUN's graduate course, I listened as the professor gave statistics indicating his expectation that about half of the class would not finish the term. He instilled some doubt in me about my skills, but two years later, I had not only made it through his class, I had earned my degree. I had relied on the perseverance I'd developed as an immigrant to expand my output to that needed for achieving the high level results I was used to. The successful completion of my graduate program along with my observations of the legal dramas at Earthlink steered me in a new direction, corporate law.

I had been introduced to this field in undergraduate Business Law. I enjoyed reading and researching cases dealing with topics such as UCC codes and principal/agent law. I was enthralled by the material and confident and powerful in expressing my views. In my graduate work, I took International Business Law taught by Professor Kurt Saunders. The class format allowed me to delve deeply into case material and legislation, which sparked my curiosity, and I was again extremely engrossed in the legal material. I pursued my interest further by enrolling in an Entertainment Law class and a new elective, an E-Commerce Law class.

When I reviewed the offerings of the law program at Southwestern University, classes focusing on such issues as agency law and property rights attracted me because such knowledge will combine well with my business background and prepare me for a career in corporate law. Gender and racial issues and the law also interest me, and I believe that with my background as an immigrant to the US, I will be able to help others on a pro bono basis or through agencies that provide services to those new to the United States. Clubs such as the Public Interest Law Committee at Southwestern University interest me because of their involvement in and support of the community.

In summary: I believe that law school is my next step toward a long-term career goal and that with my personal, educational, and corporate foundation, I will succeed academically. I have learned to organize myself well, to study effectively, to use the help of others wisely and to apply new knowledge to deepen my learning. My first-hand view of the new legal issues relating to information technology and the Internet makes me certain that I want to focus my legal career in this area. Moreover, my diverse social and cultural background will be of great benefit to me in law school and as a lawyer working and living in California's global community.

As an immigrant, I am driven to excel and to give my best in everything I do, whether that means raising challenging issues for professors and fellow classmates to consider, deeply considering the issues others raise or applying knowledge to real-life situations. I look forward to studying at Southwestern University and to becoming a useful and proud alumnus.

Sample 9

Accepted at Golden Gate University, Chapman University, and other schools; wait-listed at Santa Clara University and University of San Diego

When I was a little girl, my family lived in a small basement apartment next to the college my dad was attending in Iowa City. During the heavy winter storms, the basement would flood, and I would sit at the top of the stairs next to the door that led to the first floor, staying dry until my dad came home to "rescue" me. With little income and no relatives or support network in this new place, times were not easy for my family then, but I vividly remember that my dad always returned home from school late at night with bags full of books. Rather than "rescuing" me, he would simply squeeze into a spot next to me on the stairs and spread out his books so he could continue studying. When I looked at him with dismay, he would say, "Studying hard and working hard is the only way to get us out of the flood." He did indeed succeed in building a better life for us—his accomplishments made even more remarkable by the fact that he had grown up in a dirt-floor house in Taiwan with seven siblings and no father. With my dad's words constantly in my mind, I have always worked hard to achieve my dreams, though I had no idea then that my dream one day would be to enter Santa Clara University School of Law and even possibly SCU's JD/MBA program. My background and experiences, from those early days in the basement to my life now in the Bay Area, all combine to lead me to a career that bridges technology, law, and business.

Growing up, I knew that I had to assimilate into American society in order to succeed; however, like many new immigrants, my parents continued to send me to Chinese language, dance, and art classes, which made me feel even more separate from my peer group. The first time I felt completely uninhibited by language and cultural barriers was when I took my first computer class in high school, and later earned a summer engineering internship. I soon discovered that with computers, I could easily put my thoughts and ideas into action through universal programming languages, and realized that computer technology is something people from all cultures and backgrounds can share. Today, after obtaining a higher degree in Computer Engineering and working with technological advances at major corporations, I am a "technophile"; I cannot imagine a life that does not involve advanced technology.

In college, I was excited to get my first hands-on experience at a startup company, Imago, which developed wireless games for mobile devices. Unfortunately, my internship ended abruptly when the company collapsed, like many other dot coms. Sensing an opportunity, however, I volunteered to become part of the "idea forming committee," all that was left of Imago. I assisted with new program development, and worked closely with one of Imago's partners, Verizon, to expand their "Fun & Games" section. With a turn of events, Imago re-emerged under the new name, EbiSoft, and rewarded my loyalty by hiring me full time when I graduated. In my role as software developer, I was able to leverage my technical expertise, but our team's efforts were sometimes hindered when we had to wait days before getting a response to questions regarding intellectual property because EbiSoft could not afford an onsite lawyer. At that time, I started thinking about the tremendous benefit that comes with wearing many hats: though collaboration is very important, sometimes one person with integrated technical, legal, and business training can have a significant impact on the various aspects which lead to the success of a company.

At the end of my first year out of college, I knew I wanted to delve deeper into engineering. Thus, I parted with EbiSoft to return home and pursue a Master's degree at Santa Clara University. Attending SCU was ideal for me because I knew I would also get a chance to explore other areas that had sparked my interest since my days at EbiSoft. I was able to take some courses that helped me understand the role of intellectual property law in developing technologies, and I even had the chance to sit in on Professor Schneider's introductory law classes. Soon, my fascination with the corporate world grew to encompass the laws and processes that assist in the development of technology. One day after my IP class, as I was passing Bannan Hall and going to my car, I realized that I was finally sure that I wanted to apply for law school. I was slightly embarrassed, though, when a couple of students in the hallway saw me jump and smile to myself for no apparent reason!

Another reason why I returned home was to assist my parents, because they too had been affected by the economy's downturn. Like me, my mother had also been working at a startup company. Unfortunately, due to bad business decisions, the company failed. My father, on the other hand, had been working for the global powerhouse Enron for close to 20 years; as someone who was brought up in a family whose values emphasized honest hard work, righteousness, and honesty, I was furious to see the Enron scandal unfold, especially since it affected my dad and his friends. Through my conversations with my father, I came to realize that the Enron scandal was able to happen because of a lack of effective, enforced laws. My frustration with his situation enhanced my desire to pursue a degree that will allow me to understand the law, see both its strengths and weaknesses, and gain the power to make improvements or at least advocate changes in the corporate world. Moreover, to be an effective advocate in the corporate world, I also need to understand the inner workings of a company, namely its business practices. Thus, I may consider applying for the joint JD/MBA program later on.

To help support my parents and pay for my tuition, I worked full-time at Netquip Systems during the day and attended SCU full-time during the evening. Though times were tough, not only did I learn incredible time management skills, but I also greatly enjoyed and learned a lot from my experience at Netquip.

I got to work as part of a proof-of-concept team, evaluating the latest technology ranging from emergency tracking technologies to automated response systems to markup language conversion. What made working in the proof-of-concept lab particularly fascinating was that I had the opportunity to interact with a very diverse group of people. My most memorable recollection from my time at Netquip involves my efforts to teach a software developer how to test and interconnect networking systems; she did not have the experience working with hardware devices, so I tried to explain the theory behind computer networking in different ways, using simple analogies and drawing out diagrams. Still, she was confused. It was only when I decided to repeat all my explanations and drawings in Mandarin, that she finally felt comfortable with the hardware devices and the configuration procedure. Patience, cultural sensitivity, interpersonal skills and the ability to explain very technical subjects in an easily understood way are skills I know I will definitely need when I enter IP law.

One day during my time at Netquip, when I was helping to install wireless equipment for a showcase, it dawned on me how wonderful this complex system was; it enables us to roam freely, fully connected to the Internet, with our handheld devices. I continued to envision the role I would play if I were in IP law already. I had a lot of idealizations about what I could do: as a "one-woman band," I could help develop, market, and protect such wonderful innovations as this one. However, I wanted to get a realistic picture of what I could really achieve, so that same day, I requested a meeting with the Vice President of the Worldwide Patent Counsel Group at Netquip Systems. He reaffirmed for me that lawyers with technical knowledge are very much in demand. He also whole-heartedly encouraged me to follow the path I was considering, telling me that my experiences and background have clearly prepared me well to enter the field of law. Not long after our talk, I parted with Netquip to concentrate my efforts on achieving this transition.

Santa Clara University is where my initial interests grew into my passion, and where my passion will hopefully become reality. I would truly like to be part of Santa Clara University School of Law because of its prestigious High Technology Law program, as well as the potential for me to enter the JD/MBA Combined Degree program, which will provide me the extensive knowledge, skills, and background I need to succeed in today's dynamic markets. As I was completing my Master's degree, I fell in love with SCU because of its environment and its wealth of resources. Professor Schneider highly recommended SCU to me that day after class; he said that the School of Law has always and continues to pursue excellence in an intellectually diverse learning community dedicated to the training of professionals. From this candid dialogue, I know SCU will continue to be my "stairs out of the basement" as I climb towards my career goals. This time, I will not need to look to my dad to rescue me—it will be through my own hard work that I finish climbing the stairs and get my foot into the door.

Sample 10

Accepted at University of Florida Levin College of Law, Florida State University College of Law, and Florida Coastal School of Law

Buzz . . . Buzz . . . Buzz . . . "Ouch!"
Feeling a sharp pain, I thought of the scene in "The Marathon Man" in which Dustin Hoffman is tortured by the Josef Mengele character who is disguised as a dentist. I ended up calling the State of Florida Board of Health and eventually filed a case against this dentist with the Florida State Board of Dentistry. It took two years of following through on my part, but the Board found that my pain had been the byproduct of an unnecessary root canal performed by someone without a license to do so. On the upside, the whole experience triggered my thoughts about becoming a lawyer.

When I was a young child, my family moved throughout New Mexico but eventually ended up in the Wichita, Kansas area, where I attended middle school and high school and ended up having a relatively normal adolescence. I was enrolled in a college-prep Catholic high school, St. Francis of Assisi, where I received a top-quality education and made some really great friends. Unfortunately, the football team was recruited so the school could win state championships and I had to satisfy my craving for competitive sports by playing soccer and basketball in the local city leagues and golf with my brother on the weekends. Times got a little rough when my dad lost his job, so I worked two to three times a week at a local Mexican restaurant. Being on my feet all night after a long day at school was hard, but I was able to pay my monthly car payments and still save some money to spend.

In school, I had a knack for math and science, but found the most interesting subjects to be history, economics, and government. It was in Mr. Kito's senior economics class that I was first introduced to personal finance. My partner, Susan, and I excelled in the group project, the creation and semester-long management of a portfolio of stocks. We had the highest investment return in the class. The whole experience later influenced my choice of a major.

When I began the University of Florida in Gainesville, however, I did so as an engineering major. A Bright Futures Scholarship paid for my tuition. When I found myself reading investment books, investing my own money, and thinking realistically about my future, I changed my major to finance. Although I didn't enjoy the required business courses, which were taught on TV, I found upper level finance courses enjoyable. I loved the discussions with my teachers and classmates, finding that I definitely learn better in an interactive environment.

Meanwhile, I became very active in my fraternity and enjoyed doing many things with its 130 active members and holding many positions. I was especially pleased to be chosen as a member of our internal disciplinary board, because of my fairness and open-minded decision-making. Currently, as vice president, I handle the fraternity's financial dealings, determining its budget and managing its three employees. I established a new collections system and drafted new contracts for membership agreement.

While I was home from school one summer, I started considering all these experiences. A business law course was one of my classes that most interested me. Being actively involved in the case against the "Mengele" dentist, I considered becoming a lawyer as a possibility. Testing this idea out, last summer I was an intern in a real estate law firm and enjoyed preparing various closing contracts and sitting in on the actual closings.

Refining my interests more, I realize that I enjoy various forms of business law that deal with contracts, from corporate, real estate, trust, estate, and even intellectual property law. I am also very much interested in becoming a JAG lawyer for one of the branches of the military after I graduate law school. Aside from the enjoyable idea of traveling around the country and world and from the satisfying idea of serving in the military, the JAG corps offers professional opportunities unavailable to most new law graduates. In the corps, young lawyers are immediately given their own cases, unlike in law firms in which the novice lawyer researches for someone else. Another attractive benefit is that JAG lawyers handle every type of case. They are the defense and prosecutors for criminal cases, they handle the military's real estate, tort claims, and international law, and they handle soldier's law related to questions such as wills, trusts, and bankruptcy.

I think that the University of Florida is an excellent choice for me because it provides a good match for my interests, skills, and career goals. The International Trade Law curriculum interests me and may be something I would pursue, particularly because of my interest in becoming a JAG lawyer. The Corporate Law program also appeals to me as it lines up well with my undergraduate degree in finance. One of my top priorities is that I will remain in Gainesville, a city that I have enjoyed immensely in the past four years. With the knowledge that I will gain at the University of Florida and my own fair-mindedness and sense of responsibility, I know I will become a fine lawyer, the kind of lawyer that people will respond to with a hearty thanks rather than an alarmed "Ouch!"

Sample 11

Accepted by Cornell University Law School and Georgetown University Law Center

I sat among students of law, computer science, education, and information technology management—that diversity alone captivated me as I started the two classes, "The Internet: Business, Law, and Strategy" and "Internet Commerce and the Information Economy," at the Kennedy School of Government, where I was pursuing a master's degree. I quickly grew fascinated by the conceptual and practical challenges of defining and protecting intangible assets such as patents, brands, and copyrights; challenges that I hadn't appreciated until I directly examined them.

There were many moments in those two courses when I felt as if I were exploring the true essence of information technology—the interface of the actual technology and the society that creates and uses it. I undertook one of my final projects on cyber laws and regulations, working with my "multidisciplinary" classmates. With my science background, I quickly grasped the perspectives of my teammates in computer science and IT management and reciprocated with the international perspective and regulatory framework I had acquired through my master's studies.

From my college years to that moment, I had explored and enjoyed various professional avenues—finance, business policy, and science—but had been unable to "nail" my career direction with the gut certainty that I wanted. These classes changed that. I discovered that the field of intellectual property (IP) needs multidisciplinary individuals such as myself, and in turn can provide an incredibly rich, intellectually stimulating career through which I can make a meaningful contribution to society.

At first, as a junior at Dartmouth, I took my father's advice to follow in his footsteps and earn a doctoral degree in science. I was accepted to two doctoral programs, Penn and Tufts. I initially decided on Penn but then soon declined, because I realized that although I had the capability, I lacked the true passion for biology. Thus, upon graduation in 1997, I explored three career tracks throughout my first post-college year. I first became a freelance writer for several non-profit newspaper organizations in Seoul, Korea. I then interned at Ernst & Young Management Consulting and at Merrill Lynch Private Client Group to learn about the consulting and financial service industries. Each experience was interesting in its own right, yet none of them was fully engaging. I continued my search for a long-term career focus, an act that was painful financially and emotionally.

Part of that search was my study of policy at Harvard Kennedy School, as I felt that policy was a dimension missing from my practical and intellectual framework of business and science. At Harvard, I expanded my analytical framework and started to acquire leadership and advocacy skills. I also undertook Harvard Business School coursework to understand private management perspectives in finance and technology entrepreneurship. And I took the two classes that changed my life. My final project, which compared the IP laws of Germany, China and the US, further affirmed my interest. Suddenly, my career direction was clear—after my struggle, it happened as naturally as could be.

Upon my graduation in 2000, I joined Silicon Image, a chip design house in Silicon Valley, as a financial analyst and planner. I developed financial models to measure the value of the company's IP licenses. Our company had a broad IP portfolio but lacked capital to expand its commercialization and market penetration. Clearly, licensing our patented technology to other companies was the only way to survive during the industry downturn in 2001. I saw that IP played a strategically crucial role at our company.

In the summer of 2001, I accepted an offer from Samsung Electronics Asia-Pacific HQ in Singapore as an Assistant Manager and was promoted to Business Development Manager in April 2002. During my 14-month-stay in Singapore, I initiated strategic partnership talks with three influential organizations in Singapore: Singapore Council of Woman Organizations, Nike SE Asia HQ, and National University of Singapore. With my team's support, I successfully formed official partnerships with two of them, and one of the partnerships eventually won Asia-Pacific HQ a company award among seven regional HQs in 2002. I also implemented marketing communication activities for successful brand management. Brand, an intangible property, is the only asset that a company with many competitors can monopolize. As I have learned, rising global manufacturing standards with fluent technology and capital flow from one nation to another inevitably propel a company to protect such an intangible property as brand. Through this initiative, I gained practical experience with the phenomenon of brand, which increased my interest in protecting intangible properties.

Recently, I joined Samsung Electronics America Digital Information Technology in Irvine, California as a Strategic Marketing Manager. I utilize my analytical background for competitive analyses in seven digital product groups and manage relationships with a distributor. For the last three years, Samsung Electronics has been one of the top five companies in the number of the US patents for technology. Due to patent issues, we cannot enter certain product markets in the US that we entered in the Far East many years ago. On the other hand, many competitors cannot introduce products similar to ours despite their capabilities to make them. I consequently observe the critical relationship of patents to sales and marketing.

This recent work experience affirms my commitment to pursuing a career in intellectual property, potentially in international contexts. My goal is to become a multifaceted IP professional—one who has the skills, knowledge and license to practice IP law, but who also is able to manage the business aspects and who thoroughly understands related technologies. After law school, I plan to work for a major law firm that excels at IP law and build expertise. After several years, leveraging the multidisciplinary nature of IP, I hope to establish an IP specialty firm, starting with law and eventually expanding to include finance, business development, and marketing. When fully recognized as "the IP expert" many years later, I would like to perform policy roles in the US government.

Curiosity has driven me to diverse areas academically and professionally. An academic experience ignited my passion for IP while my work experience has deepened my skill base for becoming an IP attorney. Cornell Law School excels in both intellectual property and international law. This dual excellence of Cornell Law School will train me to become a successful IP legal professional who is internationally competitive and contributes to the development of the field.

Sample 12

Accepted at Golden Gate University School of Law

When I was two years old my mother and father separated, and my mom decided to move to Butte, Montana, where she would have better career opportunities as well as a better environment in which to raise me. As a child living in Montana, I spent my days cross-country skiing and fishing, and quickly learned to appreciate the beauty of the wilderness. It was also during these years that I decided I wanted to attend college.

I returned to the New York area when I was eighteen, moved in with my grandmother, and attended Brooklyn Heights Community College, and then New York State University, Staten Island (NYSUSI). At NYSUSI I joined a co-ed business fraternity, Beta Delta Beta, where I served as Social Chair, Secretary, and Treasurer. In these leadership roles, I was responsible for planning, organizing, and facilitating activities and events for the fraternity. While attending undergraduate school, I also worked part-time as a Customer Service Representative for Target Telemarketing Company. These commitments forced me to prioritize and allocate my time appropriately, skills that I continue to apply in my everyday life.

In 2002, I became the only person in my family to graduate from college. Graduating from NYSUSI brought me a lot of pride and joy, and I believed the world was mine. As graduation neared, I sought a position in my field of study, Human Resources Management. I secured a position with Marriott Buffalo, and began work immediately after graduation. While working for Marriott, I utilized my legal, interviewing, and organizational skills to complete a variety of human resources tasks, including interviewing, training, and providing career advancement advice to employees. Within eight months I was promoted to Senior Human Resources Representative. After a year and a half of working in Buffalo, I moved back to Montana to take a position with Butte County, where I would get more diverse human resources experience. I remained with the County for six years, and was consistently promoted to increasingly higher-level positions during my tenure there.

In July 2002, I joined Toastmasters, Inc. in Butte and became the Vice President of Public Relations. During my year as the Vice President of Public Relations, I increased our membership by fifteen percent. I earned my CTM (Competent Toastmasters) designation by completing ten core speeches with topics ranging from humor to working with props. My involvement in Toastmasters provided me with an opportunity to receive positive reinforcement and constructive feedback on my presentation skills. Also in 1998, I purchased my first home. At the age of 29, I became the youngest person in my family to own a home. As a homeowner, I served the Homeowners Board as the Secretary, where I had the opportunity to shape our CC&R's and to voice my opinion about proposed projects.

In my current position as a Human Resources Manager, I'm responsible for responding to and investigating EEOC and DFEH complaints. I also respond to all Unemployment Claims and represent the company at unemployment hearings. I represented the company by presenting our case to the Labor Commissioner for a wage and hour dispute we received by a former employee. I enjoy this aspect of my job and the challenge of determining the truth, uncovering inconsistencies, and rectifying them. I work closely with our attorney, who has told me that I complete the majority of his work since I actually write the response in the required format of allegation, statement, and facts. Once this is completed, the only items remaining for the attorney are to make minor changes and to sign the response. My interest in a career in law is a natural progression of the skills I have developed in my current position. In addition, I am currently earning my MBA at the University of Montana. I believe this experience, in addition to earning my JD, will provide me with the knowledge to assist in any legal situation that may arise.

In addition to working full-time and maintaining a 3.85 GPA in graduate school, I have also formed a Bible study at my church, which encompasses fellowship, in-depth Bible studies, social activities, and community involvement. I was also responsible for organizing a gift campaign for the County Shelter in our local community.

My above accomplishments demonstrate the contributions I will make as a student at Golden Gate Law School. As an older, minority, student, I am focused, dedicated, and full of life experiences to bring to the classroom. The faculty and the JD curriculum at Golden Gate offer exposure to various areas, including the opportunity to participate in the Workers' Rights Clinic. *[School-specific info here]* I look forward to contributing to the community at Golden Gate, and believe I will be an asset to your school both as a student and as an alumnus.

Sample 13

Accepted at Nova Southeastern University Shepard Broad Law Center

The Next Step

The picture of me that sat on my grandmother's desk wasn't some cookie-cutter school picture like most kids give their grandparents. In the photo, I am three years old, kneeling on my grandmother's desk chair, hard at "work" on the adding machine. Although I never grew up wanting to be an accountant, like she was, I did want to be just like my grandmother, and I still do.

My grandmother, Emma, died three years ago, and I experienced all the typical emotions when losing a loved one—sadness, remorse, forgiveness, maybe even relief. Perhaps more importantly, I reflected back on her life and accomplishments and evaluated the direction in which I wanted my life to head. Because of her work ethic, perseverance, selflessness, and most importantly because of the satisfaction her work gave her, my grandmother was a role model for me. She loved her job and worked at a furious pace until her death at age 82. I desire the same for myself.

My grandmother demonstrated core strengths, like dedication and endurance, that I have long tried to emulate. Learning to play the trombone at age eight, competing in music competitions in junior and senior high, performing as a drum major in the marching band, playing concerto performances in college, and now offering music instruction to children in my community comprise the last 20 years of my experience as a trombonist and musician. This lifelong dedication to music has taught me persistence and dedication in the face of failure and disappointment.

I have applied Emma's lessons of endurance and stamina to physical fitness as well. I have always been very physically active as both a cyclist and a runner, but I recently decided to challenge myself physically while also contributing to my community. In May 2002, I participated in the Shemmer Breast Cancer Three-Day, a 60-mile walk from Baltimore to Washington, D.C. I also rode in the Wilton-Simmons AIDS Foundation bike ride from North Carolina to Washington, D.C., in which I biked over 300 miles in three days. In both cases I appealed to friends and family for their emotional and financial support and raised over $2500 for these causes.

Much as I raised the bar to meet these physical challenges, I am now ready to assume the challenge of a new career. While I have honed valuable skills in restaurant management, including handling budgets, managing people, resolving conflicts, and paying close attention to detail, I realize that I am seeking a greater challenge—law school and a career as an attorney. Through the ambient noise of a restaurant kitchen and hundreds of guests chattering through their meals, I think about my contributions to my community as well as my personal satisfaction. I know that I want an environment that is more stimulating intellectually, but I also realize that just as I love teaching music to children individually, I'm looking for an environment where I can work with people on a one on one basis. I plan to practice law as an estate and trust law attorney, so that I may help others make carefully thought out and reasoned decisions about their futures and the futures of their loved ones.

While I am certain that I could have a long and successful career in the restaurant business, I want the satisfaction and fulfillment that I believe a career in law will provide. A law school education from Nova Southeastern University Law Center will help me to achieve what I desire for myself—an education at an excellent school, as well as the opportunity to return and contribute to South Florida, where I was born. My grandmother's example of working hard at something she truly loved and believed in has inspired me, and now I am ready to follow her lead. With Emma as my example, as well as my determination and will to succeed, I believe I have the key elements to become a successful attorney.

Sample 14

Accepted at University of the Pacific McGeorge School of Law and five other law schools

As a child, one of my closest friends was a boy who lived alone with his grandmother. Their house was located in a dying neighborhood whose prosperity, along with the rest of Detroit, was tied to the declining automobile industry. In an effort to restore the city and stimulate revenue, the city earmarked their neighborhood for a new shopping center and high-rise condominiums. They were given one year to move out before demolition began. My friend's grandmother resisted the city's efforts by writing local congressional members and attending city council meetings. Despite her best efforts, they were forced to move and leave their home.

At the time, I was too young to understand what was happening. When I was old enough to comprehend the situation more fully, I had seen enough of poverty to decide that I would never be in a similar position. I attended Central Michigan University, where I majored in Management Information Systems and Corporate Finance. Upon graduation, I accepted a job from Eli Lilly where I was promoted twice within three years, eventually becoming a project system team leader. After my work at Eli Lilly, I became an SAP consultant, a position in which I experienced similar professional success.

During my years at Eli Lilly, I worked closely with corporate attorneys. I found the legal work both interesting and challenging, and with my background in business, decided it would be natural for me to attend law school and embark upon a career in corporate law. Simultaneously, during my five year tenure in the business world I became aware that something was missing from my professional life, and so began volunteering at local charitable agencies. I worked at a local food bank and volunteered for various church-sponsored activities, including delivering meals to the needy and helping build homes for low-income families.

Through these experiences, I observed many instances of injustice to which the poor are subject. Often, such people fall prey to unscrupulous landlords and employers because they are unaware of their legal options. For example, I delivered meals in the dead of winter to find that the occupants of an apartment lacked heat because the landlord was reluctant to pay for the cost of repairing the heating system. On another occasion, I discovered an immigrant working for an employer who compensated her less than the legal minimum wage. Though I had initially begun my career in business to remove myself from this environment, I saw that it was people such as these, rather than corporations, who truly needed my assistance.

A degree in law would enable me to provide people with the kind of legal representation necessary to secure their basic rights. After five years in the business world, I feel that my talents would be best served, not by saving Fortune 500 companies millions of dollars as a consultant or corporate attorney, but by assisting the less fortunate as a legal advocate. Upon completion of a law degree, I would like to join an organization like Legal Aid, where my efforts will directly serve the interests of the disadvantaged and disenfranchised. My career choices are no longer about money or success, as I have already achieved both, but rather about making a difference in the lives of those who need it most.

Sample 15

Accepted at Indiana University (Bloomington) School of Law, Seton Hall University School of Law, and four tier-four law schools

How I survived elementary school without being bullied, I will never understand. While my buddies were dreaming of becoming police officers or firemen, I dreamed of being a lawyer. And as my friends donned their Jams and collected their Spiderman lunch boxes, I, much to my parents' chagrin, insisted on wearing a tie and sweater vest to my elementary school. While my parents always supported my idiosyncratic desires, they absolutely drew the line at the briefcase that I requested for my birthday. As I matured I started wearing jeans and playing sports, but I never outgrew that little lawyer that lives inside me.

Now that I am old enough for the tie and briefcase, I am ready to embark on my legal career and have decided to focus on environmental and international law. I am an avid outdoorsman, and love horseback riding, SCUBA diving, and hiking. I support local organizations such as Austin's Save Our Springs Alliance, which advocates the judicious use of the natural habit surrounding Barton Springs, and national organizations such as The Nature Conservancy, that work to preserve natural resources and endangered animals. Whether rising before the sun for a green belt clean up or working on the recycling program I began in high school, I believe that protecting our environment is a way of life that requires commitment and personal responsibility. In addition, I recognize the global implications of decisions made by governments and business and believe that we are all bound to one another more than most people realize. It is the laws of today that determine the future of our planet, and I am determined to contribute to the creation and implementation of these laws.

Some of my most valuable educational experiences have occurred when I have traveled to other countries and learned about diverse people and cultures, coexistence, and tolerance. In Vienna, while working in a study group, it occurred to me that the members of the group had both everything and nothing in common. We all came from different countries and German was the only language that we had in common, but what was most significant was that we had all come together to meet the daily demands of our education, and to share the same challenges of living in a foreign city and being away from our families. However, it was in this group that I found a new family that assuaged my fears; collectively we made each other feel at home. It renewed my faith that we can live peacefully. If our microcosm shared only one common thread but still we came to understand and care for one another, then societies can follow.

It was also through my travels that I discovered my interest in foreign policy. When I graduated from high school, I had saved enough money to finance a trip to Europe. While traveling, I discovered a passion to understand other people's political outlook. Speaking with Europeans added significant depth to discussion and understanding of foreign policy. I hope to spend the summer of 2004 exploring new cultures through the University of Pittsburgh's Semester at Sea Law Program, where students live aboard a ship, studying international law and visiting countries in Asia, Africa, and Europe.

While I am currently studying German in Vienna, I am looking forward to returning home to spend the next nine months volunteering for the Americorps program. I view this as my last opportunity to serve as a full time volunteer before law school. I will be working in my hometown of Austin, Texas with Austin Free Net, a nonprofit program funded partially through the Americorps program. Through grants and donations, AFN works to provide Internet access and technology training to those who have been excluded from the technology revolution. I will be using my teaching and leadership abilities to help ensure that disadvantaged students are able to compete in computer literacy.

My commitment to volunteer work traces to my undergraduate years as well, when I focused on improving the experience of students at my university through our orientation program. After serving as an Orientation Advisor for several years, I proposed and received approval to create a special undergraduate position to enhance our orientation program. This unique program allowed me to serve in a role that only graduate students had previously done, supervising students, creating and coordinating programs, and representing the orientation program both internally and externally. I also became involved in a national organization dedicated to improving secondary education, the National Orientation Directors Association (NODA). It was my honor to sit on the board of directors of NODA as only the second undergraduate to ever hold that position in the organization's 35-year history.

My community service, involvement on campus, and dedication to assisting others has been a strong force in my life. This background, in combination with my interest in international affairs and environmental concerns, as well as my long held desire to practice law, has laid the foundation for my law school experience and career as an attorney. I plan to combine my passion for the environment with my interest in international affairs, and practice international and environmental law, perhaps working with Lawyers Without Frontiers, the Sierra Club, or ultimately for the State Department or the United Nations.

American University's strong reputation in environmental and international law, combined with the proximity to the nation's capitol, make American my top choice for law school. I am excited about not only the educational opportunities offered by American, but by the strong and numerous experiential programs available in Washington. In addition, I am excited by the resources American University offers in assisting students, such as the combined use of the WCL and the greater campus externship programs. The diverse faculty and strength of the international affairs curriculum, as well as the possibility of pursuing a dual JD and MBA program, make American University's College of Law the most appealing school for my legal education.

Sample 16

Accepted at two top-20 law schools

Law is ubiquitous, and in the courtroom or in daily activity, it permeates much of society. In addition to the practical usefulness of a law degree, my decision to attend law school stems from my interest in legal theory, as well as my perceived connection between practicing law and writing fiction.

I started writing fiction in high school, partially because I enjoyed the creative process, but also because I found it a more effective means of communication than public speaking. During my year off from college, I had the opportunity to write scripts for a theater troupe. Writing regularly, along with working with actors and an audience, solidified my interest in fiction. Writing has helped me develop patience, determination, discipline, and self-confidence. In addition, the creative process has helped me to structure my thoughts and goals.

When brainstorming, I frequently wonder how much verisimilitude is necessary for a character to cross the line from skepticism to belief. This question can also be applied to the reader in the hope of suspending disbelief. Similarly, this is relevant in the practice of law, for instance, in attempting to persuade or create doubt in a jury.

Another way to address the above question is by asking what a person *thinks* she knows in comparison to what she *actually* knows. Many times something seems clear at first glance, but under closer inspection is ambiguous. Language is a great example of this. For instance, take the term "concealed weapon." Does concealed mean not visible or undetectable? Is a weapon an item built for a specific purpose or does any object qualify? Law jumps into these questions of uncertainty and hammers out meaning. It is an interesting process of discovery, and is at the core of my interest in law as well as fiction.

I originally became curious about law during my business law course in college. Specifically, the significance and practical application of the *Soldano v. Daniels* case caught my attention. In this case, a bartender denied a person access to a telephone in an emergency. The court addressed whether or not the bartender had a duty to allow the person to make a call. I was struck by the necessity to resolve this question and also by the law's ability to successfully do so. My curiosity expanded to include theoretical aspects in my philosophy of law course.

The course covered various progressions of legal thought, as it revealed that the law is a frequently problematic, yet secure and sound, foundation of society. Is law indeterminate? Is Rule of Judges a more appropriate term than Rule of Law? Is the law gradually uncovering a preexisting natural order? I find these questions fascinating.

In addition to my college studies, I have worked as a file clerk in a law firm for the past five months and have taken a couple of paralegal courses. The former has given me confidence that I will enjoy practicing law and working in a legal environment. The latter has helped to shape my career plans. The courses offered information on the procedural basics of several law specialties. Of the covered topics, probate law was the most interesting. Will drafting was particularly appealing, as it involves directly collaborating with clients in a helping role. We also covered the basics of mediation/dispute resolution, which is probably the most compatible with my personality since it seems to be less contentious than other careers.

I believe that my legal studies, as well as my personal and professional background, have helped me prepare for law school. Also, with my interest in fiction as a lens through which I view law, I believe I will be able to make unique contributions in daily discussion with my peers. I also believe that legal training, with its rigorous curriculum and emphasis on precise writing, will help my writing improve.

Sample 17

Accepted at George Washington University Law School, Rutgers University, Temple University Beasley School of Law, and Santa Clara University School of Law; wait-listed at University of California, Hastings College of Law

For the first nine months that I lived in St. Louis, I thought I had fallen into the perfect world. My new job as Senior Associate at Hills-Hayes Associates, a nationally recognized skills training consulting firm, offered the intellectual challenge, the variety of work and the flexible work environment that reflected my professional ideal. I had just moved from the suburbs of Amarillo, Texas, to vibrant Center City St. Louis. My husband of two years was happily pursuing his dream of a career in medicine. Then the doubt crept in.

It wasn't the 60- to 70-hour workweeks that led me to second guess my job. I enjoyed throwing myself into a project and seeing the fruits of my work. Nor was it the level of challenge or variety that the job provided. I was fortunate to test and hone my writing skills, my public speaking and facilitation skills, and my analytical abilities. I worked on projects ranging from strategic planning and grant writing to process development and improvement. I even became the principal designer of "Technology Training for Nonprofits," a Hills-Hayes product that has the potential to garner national recognition as a best practice within the skills training field. Yet as my consulting career began to take off, I unexpectedly found my enthusiasm waning. The job was not feeding my soul. The passion that had drawn me into this line of work was no longer driving me, and the intellectual challenge alone did not sustain me.

My passion for social justice emerged during a visit to Miller's Place my junior year in college. Miller's Place is an emergency homeless shelter in Amarillo where volunteers prepare and serve the meals as well as join the homeless guests for dinner. It was my first opportunity to listen to the challenges and difficulties faced by the homeless directly from the individuals themselves. As I took in their stories, I felt sad, angry, and amazed all at once. Sad that these people had to live such tenuous lives. Angry that society as a whole has spent as much, if not more, energy hiding the homeless than helping them. And amazed at the creativity and ingenuity these individuals employed to create their own community and to survive.

Emotionally and spiritually moved and politically aroused by this experience, I sought out more opportunities to interact with and help those living in poverty. I continued to volunteer at the shelter and lived in Selver Park, an inner-city neighborhood in Amarillo while participating in a summer program that provided tutoring and cultivated relationships with neighborhood families. Each of these experiences deepened my understanding of and appreciation for the lives of the poor. I also learned about the network of services that help these individuals escape their difficult situations. These experiences and learning became the basis for my college thesis entitled "Homelessness, The Private Sector's Contribution." On graduation, I was so determined to personally serve the cause of social justice that I held out for a job that would allow me to directly assist low-income individuals.

This job proved to be a position as a job counselor to the homeless in Amarillo, my initial entry into the field of skills training. The work was extremely satisfying. Each day, I was able to watch change happen one person at a time. However, the simplistic attitude that had underpinned my passion for helping people in need grew more sophisticated as I daily confronted the complex realities they face. While working with clients like Mary, who needed to remain drug-free and to be employed in order to regain custody of her three children, I realized that effecting positive change is an individual as well as a community responsibility. I had devoted much energy to helping Mary find job opportunities, prepare a résumé and practice interviewing. Yet she continued to fail to show up for numerous interviews.

As a result, after six months, she still had not complied with the requirements for regaining custody of her children. Through this encounter and others like it, I recognized that individuals have to take responsibility for their actions, or lack thereof, just as the community is responsible for providing the tools and resources to aid individuals in changing their lives. I discovered that, while I am motivated by concern for the disenfranchised, I am also driven by passion for justice: my desire for every person to receive an equal chance at succeeding in life also meant an equal chance to take responsibility for the consequences of one's actions, positive or negative.

During my subsequent counseling work at a larger skills training agency, I was swiftly promoted through several administrative and managerial positions. I used my past experiences of working directly with low-income individuals to guide my work on various projects. In spite of the increasing intellectual challenge I enjoyed in developing program management and big-picture thinking skills, I missed the direct contact with the people we were seeking to help. Similarly, my current position at Hills-Hayes Associates allows me to fully explore the larger problems within skills training and devise solutions for them. Yet I never interact with the end-users of the programs, the people needing jobs and training.

About nine months ago, I noticed that my work had settled into a routine: applying variations of the same solutions to the same types of problems. The intellectual stimulation waned and along with it my interest in this work. I started longing for something new that would satisfy both my intellectual hunger and my core passion. At the same time, my husband and I decided that our marriage was no longer working. So I was now free to pursue whatever I wanted. I chose law school—though it was not a completely new idea for me.

Toward the end of my senior year in high school, my friend's father, a probate judge, told me I should become a lawyer. He said I was cut out for it because I naturally "think" like a lawyer. The seed was planted. As I moved further into management level work, the idea of attending law school surfaced more frequently. It seemed that the seed had taken root and after a long dormancy was starting to grow. So I began to explore the field of law in more detail. These explorations have led me to see that law combines the opportunity to directly impact the lives of the disenfranchised, to engage in the intellectual challenge of analyzing multidimensional problems and finding solutions, and to promote justice. Within the field of law, I am intrigued by three specific areas that address my desire to help the less fortunate and to promote justice. Family law, particularly that involving youth or domestic violence, would allow me to assist individuals who are facing significant life challenges. Advocacy work would position me to speak on their behalf. Working in a district attorney's office would give me a practical means to advance the principle of individuals taking responsibility for their actions.

It is the right time for the seed of a dream that was planted so many years ago to finally come to fruition. I am appreciative that my work along the way, while having its ups and downs, enabled me to develop skills that will be valuable when I become an attorney. I realize that no job is perfect or ideal, but I also realize that I need to be directly involved in promoting justice and personally engaged in the practical, intellectual, and political challenges of doing so.

Sample 18

Accepted at San Francisco Law School; wait-listed at University of San Francisco School of Law

In July 1996, I was named as a primary defendant in a lawsuit filed by the purchaser of my condominium, who claimed that I had failed to disclose a defective roof prior to close of escrow. He charged me with fraud, negligence, and nondisclosure and sought a half million dollars in damages and lost wages. I was stunned by such a charge. Never before had I been sued and I knew nothing of my legal rights. A judgment against me of this magnitude would've ruined me financially and severely disrupted my family. I also would've lost my security clearance and therefore my job.

I sought my real estate agent's advice since he was among 6 others who were named as defendants in the case. Realizing that he was liable for failure as my fiduciary, the agent recommended an attorney whose strategy was to minimize the agent's liability and legal expenses. I was originally unaware of these intentions and hired him thinking that the case would only last a few months. This proved costly for me as my attorney took on the laboring oar of heading the defense of this case at my expense, responding to the frivolous motions and delay tactics of the plaintiff's counsel without insisting on a speedy resolution. To my astonishment, it took nearly a year to get to mediation at a cost of $25,000. When presented with a chance to end the case by giving the plaintiff $1500, I refused believing that such action was an admission of guilt and I firmly believed that I had done nothing wrong. At my insistence, my attorney filed a cross-complaint against my agent and a counter-suit against the plaintiff.

Over the next four years the case took a variety of legal turns, all intended to force me to settle without addressing my claims before an arbitrator. I would spend another $70,000 before finally prevailing in two separate arbitration sessions and winning both the counter-suit and the cross-complaint. This was a sustained effort that required my commitment while I was working a demanding software job.

My involvement in this lawsuit uncovered a love for the law that I didn't know existed and this was evidenced by my deep participation in every aspect of the case. Suspicious of my attorney's motives, I separately consulted with 12 attorneys throughout the case to discuss the suitability of my attorney's legal tactics, and to educate myself on my legal options, those of the plaintiff, and those of my real estate agent. Their professionalism and knowledge fascinated me and I admired the power that they held in affecting people's lives. I proofread every motion and response that my attorney produced. I researched contract law as it pertained to real estate transactions and the duties of a fiduciary. At mediation I recognized that the plaintiff's case had no merit and that he was willing to settle for less than $10,000 despite his attorney's dramatics. I also recognized that my attorney's reluctance to mention the filing of a cross-complaint against my real estate agent for failure in his fiduciary duties was a clear indication that he was determined to minimize the agent's legal expenses. Despite my attorney's opinion that we had absolutely no chance to win, I insisted on filing a motion to contest a good faith settlement between my agent and the plaintiff because this would've released the agent from any liability to me. My late night editing of the legal argument for this motion contributed to our winning it. I kept my attorney on the case until we prevailed against the plaintiff in arbitration. I then released him because of his refusal to prosecute the real estate agent. I hired another attorney to handle the cross-complaint against the agent. During arbitration, I produced evidence that conflicted with the testimony of the agent's key witness, himself an attorney, forcing the witness to change his testimony, which sealed our victory. My decision to bring the evidence came without my attorney's knowledge and was done in anticipation of the legal tactics of the agent's counsel. In essence, I had discovered a reason for returning to school and my passion for the law.

For 20 years, I have been eager to return to school to reestablish the high academic credentials that I enjoyed prior to college. My dismal, but uncharacteristic, undergraduate performance was a prelude to a difficult future, one that required me to prove my mettle with each turn. Possessing an undergraduate degree from a prestigious university, a low GPA, and no job prospects, I did not receive my first job until nearly two years following my graduation. To obtain this job, I embarked on a course of self-study that required 6 months of sustained effort, developing a portfolio to prove to potential employers that I was indeed far more capable than my academic record indicated. The portfolio consisted of a massive software program to automate a bowling alley. This was a class project at which I had failed miserably. It was important for me to complete this assignment. I chose to implement this project in a computer language I had failed to learn while in school. I made a development schedule for myself and stuck to it. I was careful to illustrate each stage of the development, showing that I had a command of the software lifecycle. After 4 months, I was granted an interview at two Defense contractors, and upon showing them this nearly completed portfolio, I received my only two offers. Aside from convincing others that I was capable, the portfolio reaffirmed my belief that there was no concept that was beyond my grasp when I am focused. I also wanted to show that I could sustain a software development effort, creating a solution that not only worked, but one that demonstrated the quality of work that I am capable of producing and the methodical manner in which I can produce it. This would be a trademark for me throughout my career: dedication; perseverance; resourcefulness in the face of adversity; quality of work; willingness to do whatever it takes to accomplish a task and meet expectations. These are qualities well suited for the study of law.

For 17 years, I have worked for four Defense contractors as a software engineer in positions of increasing responsibility, and my foundation in technology bodes well for the contributions that I can make to legal areas that involve intellectual property. I have held a top-secret security clearance during this time, adhering to the highest ethical standards. To maintain the clearance, I had to agree to uphold and safeguard the most sensitive information vital to the national security of this country. Every 5 years, I had to undergo a polygraph test, an extensive background investigation, and be evaluated to determine if I was psychologically and mentally capable of being in such a trusted position. Under these circumstances, I have contributed my software expertise to over 20 projects and I have done whatever was necessary to make effective contributions to encourage the success of each company that I have been fortunate to be a part of. I have been dedicated enough to work 80-hour weeks and weekends to accomplish my tasks. My software engineering responsibilities have also required that I do what is necessary to remain technically current in the ever-changing world of technology through self-study. It has required that I learn how to be a team contributor as well as a team leader and motivator. It has also required that I make technical presentations, which required learning how to be a more effective and persuasive communicator. Professionally, I have been employed in a software related occupation that required me to: speak in support of a product; provide instruction related to product efficiency and effectiveness; acquire knowledge related to a product or a situation surrounding a product; speak with ease and authority related to a product; and develop logical methodologies to address product deployment and/or product problems. In other words, I have been a successful advocate, advisor, researcher, communicator, and strategist in the software industry, skills that are necessary for a career as an attorney.

In addition, it is time for me to apply my writing skills and people-oriented nature as well as my analytical skills. Throughout my life, my writing has received recognition, but I largely ignored this talent. My English papers were frequently read aloud as excellent models, including in my college creative writing class. In college, I never got below a B on any paper. As a software engineer, I wrote extensive technical documentation, often cited as effectively conveying the true intent of the software, and making it easier for other engineers to modify my software without my being present. One contractor asked me to write a technical manual even though a separate technical writing department existed for this purpose. In the lawsuit, my comments and critiques of the legal briefings and responses as well as my correspondence with all the attorneys I consulted proved vital in framing the direction of the case to my benefit. It is now a great desire of mine to be a writing attorney, one who is capable of telling stories with a legal perspective and a range that encompasses growing up in a working-class section of a small town near Chicago amidst friends who are now dead, in jail, or addicted to illegal drugs and alcohol.

Knowing first-hand the importance of contributing to community activities, I volunteer in teaching the violin to children and instructing children and adults in the martial art of Tae Kwon Do at a local community center. In teaching the violin, I have been quite effective in determining what aspect of classical music motivates each student. I take great interest in enriching the imaginations of these kids by exposing them to the same classical composers that influenced me as a child. Similarly, teaching martial arts requires the ability to recognize and regulate the limitations and strengths of individuals in a group. In both volunteer activities, I have the chance to inspire by example. I intend on using the skills that I have learned relating to children and adults to effectively communicate as an attorney.

I compare my discovery of this intense interest in the law and of my potential to excel in it as an attorney to the moment when I was given a chance to learn the violin. I was in second grade when a music teacher introduced the violin, viola, and cello to my class. When I heard it, I got goose bumps. I would go on to embrace this instrument and it became a lifelong passion. When I first received my violin, I would play it endlessly and preferred it to any other activity. I was so captivated by the violin that when it was not in my possession, I would think about it. I would go on to play first violin in four orchestras and perform for audiences. It has been 35 years and I still hold the same love for the violin. Such is the case with law and my commitment to the legal profession if I am given the chance to participate. Just as the consulting attorneys I found positively impacted my life, my greatest desire as I look forward a few years is to have a similar positive impact on others.

Sample 19

Accepted at the University of Hawaii Richardson School of Law

I have a history of making career and life decisions based partly on instinct and partly on good luck. When I graduated from college, I had an accounting degree from Stanford and a job offer from Ernst & Young. I felt confident that my future looked secure and well organized. But instead of taking the Ernst & Young job, I chose to move to Hawaii and work with my husband in our own company. I got my MBA in finance by commuting to USC and became certified as a Chartered Financial Analyst (CFA). While it wasn't necessarily the straight and narrow path I had originally conceived, the decision turned out to be a lucrative one. Our investment advisory firm, Los Verdes Partners, grew from $20 million to $450 million under our management in 10 years. This was fortunate, because after 10 years and three daughters together, my husband and I divorced.

Based on my experience and education regarding investing, I recognized that it is difficult to consistently outperform the market by selecting individual stocks. I concluded that if investing is not a hobby, one is better off having a good top-level asset allocation strategy and investing the equity position in no-load mutual funds. These beliefs led to the decision to take a break from the stock market. While I reorganized my goals, I taught surfing at Oahu Sports for the next three years. Teaching surfing led to interests in other sports, including a newfound interest in horseback riding and golf. While this was a healthy occupation, I knew teaching surfing wasn't a path I wanted to stay on for life.

Returning to my accounting roots, I took a job with Dolane Logistics as an analyst in the accounting department. Within a year I was the Corporate Controller, reporting to the Vice President of Finance, and consolidating the financial and operating statements for the three divisions of the company. It was a huge growth period for Dolane. We added two divisions and I was traveling and working over 60 hours a week for five years. When we were bought out in May 2002, I was part of the small top corporate team that was let go. Happily, this was perfect timing for me, as I had gotten remarried and was preparing to go on maternity leave with my son.

But instead of taking time off with my new baby and going back into corporate finance, I decided to follow another path and go into real estate. I mortgaged an apartment that I owned, bought six investment properties, and got my real estate license. Again, my decision to try my hand at something new paid off. Real estate has been outstanding in Hawaii, and in the past two years, I have completed 15 agent transactions and made 100% on my investments. I'm also teaching escrow servicing for my company and advanced real estate marketing in the graduate program at the University of Oahu.

I enjoy working in real estate, but now feel like I want to do more. I would like to combine my experience with an understanding of the legal system and estate planning in Hawaii. Instead of just looking at a client's investments or real estate portfolio, I want to put together a complete package and help structure efficient estates. My background should give me an advantage in dealing with the financial details of people's lives.

While I may be making another turn in my career path, it is a logical progression. I have accumulated experience extremely helpful to becoming an effective and well-versed estate planner. My acquired analytical skills will enable me to master the material in the classroom and my thorough understanding of finance, accounting, and real estate should help me to better assess clients' estate planning needs. My instincts have proven correct in the past and hopefully they will be accompanied again by good luck and I will be offered the opportunity to achieve this goal by studying at the Richardson School of Law.

Sample 20

Accepted at Whittier College Law School

Every morning, heated negotiations await me on the phones and in my office at Millennium Transportation. As a freight broker, I am engaged with customers and carriers who are trying ceaselessly to increase their profit margins. The concept is simple: book freight at the highest price and move it at the lowest. What's left is yours to keep. I must be careful not to alienate either side, which is always difficult when finance and revenues are involved. Brokering is quite a contrast to my previous position in Information Technology (IT), which was conducted at a workstation with email exchanges. Both experiences have taught me how to communicate well, whether it is in writing, in person or over the phone. I believe that my communication and negotiation skills, combined with my ability to establish good working relationships with others, be they blue-collar or white-collar professionals, will aid me as an Intellectual Property and Corporate Lawyer.

My interest in Intellectual Property Law began as an outgrowth of my work in IT. In 1998, shortly after I transferred to Cal State University Northridge (CSUN) as a marketing major, I accepted a sales consultant job with Earthlink Network (ELN), a company in its infancy and just budding. During my first six months as a sales agent, I fielded calls from an entire spectrum of Internet consumers wanting to know more about the World Wide Web and how to get on the Internet. The company exuded the energy of the Internet boom. During my tenure there, I experienced a new job opportunity around every corner or cubicle and held five position titles. I learned about sales, supervising, training, reporting, operations, project management, workforce management, forecasting and call center operations. I enjoyed the way database objects have multiple solutions and the way designing databases is subjective in nature since there are several logically sound ways to address any problem. In one database project I managed, a key field tied to a process had two definitions or values, which was a problem. With some trial and error, we changed the design from its original form into a new working form and experienced no change to the output. The experience was a prime example of how logic can be successfully applied to a problem that seems unsolvable.

Many of the projects I worked on at ELN involved partnerships with outside vendors and needed approval from the company's Legal Department before we could proceed; this sparked my curiosity about the contract side of partnerships and business dealings. I first heard of intellectual property when several of my associates began purchasing domain names using celebrities' names and needed to be cautious about infringing on intellectual property rights. I began wondering about the way applying logical reasoning could protect intellectual property.

Although I concentrated on the growth and changes in my work life at ELN, I did finish my B.S. in Marketing. My involvement with the Internet boom, however, contributed to my earning only average grades. A couple of years after finishing my undergraduate work, I decided to prove to myself that I had the ability to excel in the classroom as well as at work. I started an MBA program with a concentration in IT at the University of Laverne (ULV) in January of 2003. I will be completing the work March 04, 2004. I study ahead of lectures and devote time in the evenings to reading and supplemental research and have used my MBA studies as an opportunity to reprogram old habits of academic procrastination. I attend classes and lectures with mental agility, especially enjoying those on globalization in today's developing countries and discussions of foreign direct investment, emerging markets, and outsourcing. With renewed ambition and interest in my course subjects, I have maintained a 3.85 GPA.

At ULV, we discuss the disappearance of infrastructure obstacles and telecom problems developing countries faced prior to attracting Western firms and white collar IT jobs. After a year of surviving company layoffs, my participation in the discussions included first-hand experience with the downside—I lost my job due to overseas outsourcing. Subsequently, I looked beyond my business education. I thought about seriously pursuing my interest in globalization and intellectual property.

I had paid close attention to law as an undergraduate and also in 2003 during a dispute with my HOA. At CSUN, I took a Business Law class taught by a practicing attorney who concluded each lecture by sharing some facts and details about his previous cases, which enlivened the school day for me. Studying case reviews and analyzing torts and contracts in civil and criminal law was my first formal experience with law studies. I felt that the Business Law cases were always significant in their impact on society. Later, as a homeowner, I had occasion to present a case before the city. A neighbor was in violation of a city code, infringing upon my right to a peaceful residence. This homeowner owned the unit above mine and decided to install hardwood floors, in direct violation of the CC&Rs and city code pertaining to sound attenuation. Noise from above kept me up to all hours of the night, but I couldn't force the neighbor to pull out the floors even though Glendale city code stated only wall-to-wall carpeting was permitted in the building. Although city code was precise in its sound measurements, the matter certainly required a flexible solution. All the legal and code information pertaining to the problem was available online, and I built a case to present to the HOA. Ultimately the city attorney's office determined that the wood floors in violation needed to be lifted so that padding could be installed underneath. As long as the padding met the city's sound requirements, the problem could be resolved. The dispute was resolved fairly and equally for both parties without any resentment. My neighbor was happy because she was able to keep her floors, and I was happy because the new quiet allowed me to sleep. I realized the power of justice within the confines of the legal system.

With the Internet growing as a medium and becoming a conventional part of our society, I want to aid in protecting the rights of those whose intellectual property is infringed upon by an expanding IT environment.

While reviewing Whittier's curriculum, several classes caught my eye, including Alternative Dispute Resolution. This class will expose me to the entire spectrum of negotiation beyond freight. The Computer and the Law course explores the impact the Internet has had on commercial transactions, computer crime, as well as Intellectual Property law, all of which will add to the knowledge I gained from my graduate IT coursework. The Corporations Seminar piques my interest because of its exploration into the dynamics of multimedia corporations and the insight it promises for my understanding of ELN's legal department.

With my past work experience within a progressive corporate environment, my IT training and experience, a broader educational experience with my

MBA, and a renewed sense of academic priorities, I am ready for the challenge of law school. I believe I will succeed in my studies and in accomplishing my goal of earning a JD degree. I look forward to attending Whittier and to a career contributing to society's understanding of the impact of both globalization and information technology on Intellectual Property and Corporate Law.

Sample 21

Accepted at Emory University School of Law, Southern Methodist University Dedman School of Law, University of Houston Law Center, University of Cincinnati College of Law, and University of Kentucky College of Law; wait-listed at University of Southern California Law School

After playing basketball for most of my youth, it was just another normal day in my high school gym class shooting hoops. I never expected that the events of the day would change my life forever. A chance misplacement of footing sent me tripping over a basketball, only to rise with a severe injury from which I have never fully recovered. This event, in combination with my acceptance into a summer program offered at Name University called Talent Finder America (TFA), laid the foundation for my desire to study and practice law.

TFA, designed to teach accelerated students in advanced subject matter, determined the course of my academic development. An introduction to computer programming had me hooked from the first class. Historically, I had found strength in mathematics, but wanted to study a subject with more dimension than can be found in a geometric proof or an algebraic equation. After continuing my study of computers through high school, I chose computer science as a major when I got to college. I found something pure in the type of analytical thinking one must carry out as a programmer: using and combining predefined rules in order to generate new solutions to a problem. With every increasingly challenging course, I came closer to the realization that my brain was made to think in this manner.

While computer science appealed to me cognitively, I never embraced the countless hours spent in front of a computer screen typing code. My true passion was discovered only by accident. Getting up from the gym floor that day in ninth grade, I looked down to find my left elbow bent ninety degrees backwards. My arm was very seriously fractured and my Ulnar nerve was cut, causing a loss of control to the movement of my fingers. Weeks after the initial surgery, my father came home bearing a gift—a classical guitar. By his logic, with my limited dexterity, learning to play would be the perfect rehabilitation. Although I will never have a full range of motion in my elbow, my fingers completely recovered.

Playing the guitar was not only the most successful treatment for my nerve damage, but also for my teenage angst as well, and music has been an enormous part of my life ever since. I have developed my skills for ten years, playing in bands in both Seattle and Portland. Music appeals to me because of its boundless creativity; in writing songs there are an infinite number of approaches. In contrast to the strict logical guidelines of programming, there are very few rules at all.

After taking two courses in recording engineering in college, I found a new calling. Recording provided me with a new direction to take my musical creativity, and its connection to computers made good use of my programming knowledge. I devoted most of my spare time to honing my studio skills, under directed internships at recording studios and radio shows, including comedian Vincent Pastore's "The Wiseguy Show." However, as much as I loved engineering, I still could not reconcile the long days and nights staring at a monitor. With the end of my college career in sight, I decided on a profession in which I could find a similar marriage of creativity and logic, but gave me a little more human contact.

At first glance, law appears to have nothing to do with computers or music at all. But law is a perfect union, in its own idiosyncratic way, between analytical and creative thinking. It contains the same analytical thinking involved in writing a computer program, in that in order to win an argument, a lawyer must cite a number of predefined laws and combine them in such a way as to satisfy the judge and jury. In a very different manner, law makes use of the same creative thinking a musician would encounter in songwriting; a lawyer can be creative in choosing many possible approaches to winning the case.

On a more practical level, I have been following the ongoing battle of music copyright law fervently since high school. Even before Napster, the Harry Fox Agency threatened lawsuits against individuals who distributed guitar tablature (a form of sheet music) over the Internet, thereby reducing the number of popular songs I could learn to play without buying the book at a music store. Obtaining my Juris Doctor, with a concentration in entertainment law, would give me the entrée into the music industry that I seek.

My desire to challenge myself academically, combined with my need to follow artistic pursuits, has driven me to choose a future in law practice. It always intrigues me when I glance down at the long scar on my arm, and think how, in a strange way, I'm happy that it's there. Without it, I may have never discovered what I really wanted to do with my life.

Sample 22

Accepted at Georgetown University Law Center and George Washington University Law School

The crack of the bat, the roar of the crowds—that used to be enough. Baseball was everything to me. During the summer before my senior year in high school, I played first base and pitched for a team that, after sixty games in sixty days, won the national championship. I was later recruited for several college teams, and accepted an offer to play for the University of Pennsylvania. Overall, I felt pretty satisfied with myself. Now there were just two weeks of school standing between me and another summer of baseball.

That's when it all started.

The last two weeks of school were set aside for senior projects. For my senior project, I interviewed with Senator Bill Bradley and was accepted to spend those two weeks with his non-profit think tank, the Academy of Leadership. The Academy of Leadership wrote position papers designed to influence legislation regarding education, health care, free trade, and foreign policy. Although I knew about the organization's work, I most looked forward to getting to know this Olympic athlete and former pro basketball player. I expected that Bill Bradley would be a man's man, and my next two weeks would be filled with insider sports stories that I could later recount to my friends. However, sports never once came up. Instead, it was in this atmosphere that I first discovered the intricacies of politics and law, and uncovered what would turn out to be a growing passion for the process and public interchange involved in developing legislation, as well as a fundamental belief in the importance of an education in law in accomplishing whatever it is I choose to do with my life.

Senator Bradley's ideas about national issues were very important to him and, right from the start, he expected these issues to be just as important to me. He talked with his staff for hours about our duty within the private sector and government to develop programs to help those in need. Senator Bradley was passionate about improving race relations, health care, and economic opportunity for the disadvantaged in his home state and the nation, and the most important tool he used to realize his ambitions was the law. Senator Bradley had reached the end of his athletic career and found a positive outlet for his talents and ambitions. At the time, I did not realize that those two weeks had brought me to a similar turning point in my own life.

My first year of college came and went. I played varsity baseball, took a wide variety of classes, and joined a fraternity. However, as summer approached, I discovered that, for the first time in my life, I was not excited about the upcoming baseball season. I felt unfulfilled. An emptiness had been growing throughout my freshman year, and I knew I had to do much more with my life than I had originally planned. After some introspection, I realized that I missed the exchange of ideas I had experienced during my internship. I wanted to return to politics and law, not the baseball diamond. Drastically changing my direction, I decided to spend that summer learning more about politics and law.

And so I traded my spikes for loafers. I was accepted as a summer intern with Tim Russert at NBC's *Meet the Press*. My responsibility was to research issues and positions that we knew would be taken by guests on that week's show. This required me to quickly learn a variety of new issues each week, often within only a few hours of the show, and know where to find opposing arguments to those positions. I also had to study the show itself to see if my research and the way questions were formed really got at the heart of the issue. This is what I enjoyed the most, a chance to counter the positions of that week's guests, no matter whether I thought that they were right or wrong. On Sundays, I played host to that week's guests while they were not on camera. I had the opportunity to compare the personal characteristics of other world leaders to what I had learned from Senator Bradley. I was exposed to a variety of issues and people who championed those issues, and from each of them I learned more about how they made their arguments and supported their positions. It was obvious to me that each of these people had one thing in common: each of them used the law to champion their positions.

I returned to school with a new appreciation for college. I chose my classes with excitement and declared my major in political science. However, the end of my baseball career left me with free time that schoolwork alone could not fill. I joined the Connaisance Committee at Penn, a student group that brought to campus many world leaders, politicians, journalists, and well-known personalities. I also helped organize and became a board member of Penn Students for Bill Bradley, establishing campus meetings and organizing voter registration drives for students and residents of West Philadelphia to increase awareness of issues related to the 2000 Presidential election and Bill Bradley's candidacy. Through my work with these organizations, I further developed my understanding of the debates surrounding current issues and legislation. I also discovered that I could excel intellectually outside of the classroom and that my work ethic and ideas inspired others. Again, I had found an outlet for my talents and ideas.

As my experiences grew and my aspirations changed, law and politics increased in importance. That summer I worked as a ranger for the Nantucket Marine and Shellfish Department enforcing the laws protecting wildlife and endangered species. While it seems quite humorous now, I took my civic responsibilities very seriously, and used all of my logical, rational, and persuasive powers to keep beachgoers off the beach all summer to protect the sanctuary of the protected piping plover.

Near the end of that summer, I learned a lesson in the realities of politics. I was selected as a delegate to represent Pennsylvania as a member of the Rules Committee at the Democratic National Convention. In preparation, I spent much of the summer studying issues up for a vote at the convention and preparing to debate as I had done so many times for *Meet the Press*. However, as I discovered my first night in Los Angeles, the convention was a mere formality. No issues were debated, all votes were taken within the first five minutes of breakfast, and the results seemed to be predetermined. In reality, the public participation that we are taught to believe is the cornerstone of the political process does not exist. While I realized that the convention had become more of a post-primary party, I left Los Angeles with a desire to immerse myself even further in the study of law, politics, and legislation.

The summer before my senior year, I was accepted as an intern for Senator Chuck Hagel, who is known for his expertise in world affairs, conservative domestic policy opinions, and middle-of-the-road social views. As with Senator Bradley, I again saw the interaction of law and policy. While Senator Bradley used the law to help form policy to enable social change, Senator Hagel used the same law to effect that change in a different way. From those two experiences, I became convinced that law is the most important tool, whether enacting, enforcing, or interpreting laws, of change in a free society.

The last four years have passed quickly, but in that time I have come a long way from that national championship summer. I appreciate the opportunities that baseball afforded, as I received a great education from the University of Pennsylvania and learned much from my challenging courses, but striking out a batter no longer holds the same thrill. Instead, my political and legal activities outside of the classroom have shaped my life's direction. Capitol Hill replaced the pitchers' mound as I discovered my passion for understanding and influencing the legislative process. I want to develop that passion with a law degree from the George Washington University Law School. My father's praise for his alma mater plays no small part in influencing my decision to apply for this program, but I am most interested in continuing my extracurricular learning through the Civil Litigation Clinic. The opportunity to serve the public while developing my understanding of legal proceedings promises to be a very rewarding opportunity. I do not know exactly where my passion will take me, but whether I choose business, politics, private practice, or public service, I am convinced that my understanding of the law will be the foundation of my future.

Sample 23

Accepted at Pace University School of Law

When they first arrived to America, my parents could not speak English. However, they arrived carrying their dreams of a better life for their children and their desires to succeed. Within two years my father passed his medical licensing exam and has since developed an OB/GYN practice in Brooklyn and Manhattan. His perseverance and commitment have always been a model for me.

I entered college with the intention of becoming a doctor. After all, my father was a doctor and it was presumed, expected, nay, demanded that I would follow in his footsteps. A funny thing happened along the way; my interest in economics began to dominate my focus. An international institutions course made me conscious of how the world and all its many cultures and various people can be analyzed, organized, thought about in some disciplined way.

While in college I spent a semester studying in Spain. Sitting in the living room with my host mother and her two young children, I was reminded that despite outward superficial differences, everyone strives for the same things: a liberal government, employment opportunities and a more prosperous future for their children.

Watching the news that night, there was a story about Iraq and the United Nations. It was at that moment that I realized I wanted a deeper understanding of the institutions such as the WTO, IMF, World Bank, and the United Nations that bind the world and its people to one another. I hope that law school will not only provide me with a profession to realize this goal but also with a disciplined method of observing and thinking that will enrich all my experiences.

This desire is a natural extension of many themes that have developed in my life. Coming from an immigrant Polish family and growing up in a very diversified area of Brooklyn, New York, I was exposed to people from many countries, with many interesting stories. Each summer as a child, I would go to Israel to live with my aunt. While there, I traveled with my cousins visiting Italy, France, England, Scotland, Switzerland, and other European countries.

Polish is my mother tongue and the first language that I learned. We have many Russian friends from whom I learned that language even before I spoke English. During my time in Israel, I learned Hebrew. My elementary schooling in and continued study of Spanish have made me capable in that language as well. These were the ideas that I turned around in my mind while watching that news program.

I believe that law school would give formal structure and understanding to my interest in international institutions and the economics.

Sample 24

Accepted at University of Virginia School of Law

How can a philanthropic institution ensure that the beneficiaries of its largesse reflect the values it was founded to promote? Answering that question is one of two key reasons I seek a law degree from the University of Virginia School of Law.

As the grandson of Erskine Matteson, a prominent political advisor, I grew up believing heated debates about political issues and principles were perfectly normal dinnertime fare. At the table you were not allowed to speak unless you had an opinion about President Clinton's foreign policy or the fate of New Deal ideals. Nobody belittled you because of your age or political stance, but indifference to American values was not tolerated. Sometimes I came out the loser in these debates, but they gave me my passion for politics and social values.

My grandfather was a Welsh immigrant who fell in love with America as soon as he arrived here. When he died in 1997, his will stipulated that the organization now known as the Erskine Matteson Foundation be founded to promote the principles of New Deal liberalism. In the summer of 2002, serving as a volunteer at his Foundation, my eyes were opened to the challenges faced by philanthropic institutions and the satisfactions of working for organizations that promote social ideals. Since the Foundation was still young, I had the opportunity to help create the basic framework to safeguard its longevity. I helped set up its guidelines, revise its governance documents, and establish its long-term investment criteria and objectives. Currently, as the Foundation's Director and Successor Trustee, I review submitted grant proposals, determine which proposals to fund, and decide how best to invest the Foundation's monies.

My grandfather was not a lawyer and lacked the legal knowledge to prevent abuses of his intent by the recipients of his generosity. I seek a law degree from Virginia Law so I can prevent such scenarios from occurring to the Foundation that is now fulfilling my grandfather's purpose. Although the Foundation will always be a high priority of my life, my long-term career goals center on politics. Three summers ago, serving as a legislative aide for Oklahoma State Senator Fred Quigley I gained rare insights into the operation of the political system, from analyzing public policy issues to working with a team as a political unit. When my internship was over, I knew I had found my calling. Thus, after I put the Foundation on a firm legal footing, I will—with the cooperation of the voters of Tulsa—begin a political career as a state representative. I want to implement good public policy with a special focus on educational opportunity, health care reform, and voter participation. If I am lucky, I will be in a position to make a run at Congress in fifteen years.

Many of my career aims have been served by my study in Tulane University's Masters of Social Policy program. To formulate good public policy, however, I must be able to translate my ideas into the language of law. Combined with my public policy studies, a law degree from the University of Virginia School of Law will equip me with the tools to serve my constituents well and positively impact society.

Sample 25

Accepted at University of Chicago Law School

Academics may wrangle over the theory of market efficiency, but we in the financial community face the daily reality that few active fund managers consistently earn outsized returns and that, net of fees, almost none earn even a market return. Stated plainly, few members of my profession earn their keep. In our defense, we confront an investment universe populated mostly by overpriced assets and profligate managements. Luckily, the democratic character of share ownership offers vocal share holders at least the opportunity to improve both management and their returns. Several years spent observing corporations abuse their fiduciary responsibility has taught me that, in many cases, shareholders must exercise their right to organize against management if they are to reap the fair benefits of their investment. In my impressionable youth I believed that the position of sell-side research analyst could be a vehicle to confront these abuses, but after several years there, I have come to see the law as a more direct and effective challenger.

I first began to explore the role of shareholder activist about three years ago, after reviewing the sad performance of a bank-holding company in rural Sandusky County, Ohio, that some family members and I had invested in. My careful examination of the company's SEC filings revealed efficiency and capitalization far below that of local competitors and a loan loss reserve that, curiously, always declined despite rising loans on accrual–an old cookie-jar not yet depleted. Selling out at book value seemed the wrong response, however. I knew the law offered me another option through the privileges it extends to minority shareholders, which I decided to experiment with. I felt that by improving the bank's management and financial position I would not only raise the value of my holdings, but perhaps, in a small way, improve the county's economy, which the prosperity of the last twenty years had passed over. Because the bank is the dominant (if not particularly competitive) financial institution in the county, this was not an unrealistic ambition.

My handicaps in this experiment were a relatively small ownership position, secondary status as an out-of-towner, and a board that unanimously (at least publicly) refused to admit it had under performed and adamantly opposed any change that might threaten its local stature. Moreover, the board, perhaps because it was anticipating a hostile offer, had entrenched itself by introducing staggered terms and eliminating cumulative voting from its by-laws. In my favor, was the illiquidity of the stock (traded on NASDAQ small-cap), which left many holders frustrated by years of laggard returns and willing to work with me.

I soon discovered that courteous inquiries were insufficient to motivate the firm to reform some of their more dated and inefficient procedures and thus adopted a litigious approach. Management grudgingly accepted into their proxy my first shareholder's resolution, a vaguely worded and non-binding suggestion that the board work to improve shareholder value. My request for a list of shareholders met a less genial fate though we were clearly entitled to it under both Ohio statute and case law. I had no choice but to file suit in Common Pleas and, at considerable expense to the bank, negotiate the release of the list through the largest law firm in Northwest Ohio. We were successful, and I learned a valuable lesson about the ability of court pleadings and filings to bridge the gap between intention and realization.

List in hand, I began soliciting its inhabitants for their support. Fortunately, few of this company's shares are held in street name, and I was able to easily locate and speak to many of the larger holders (there was little institutional ownership). Some refused to speak with me and others disparaged me as an "out-of-towner"—their comments sounding like dialogue from a Sinclair Lewis or Sherwood Anderson novel. I found a discouraging number who agreed with me wholeheartedly about the need for change, but who were afraid to vote against the board for fear of jeopardizing their lending arrangements.

That first resolution received only modest support, about 10% of all shares, but by sponsoring it, I was able to study the mechanics of proxy contests and the psychology of individuals who vote their proxy. It also attracted the attention of a few small fund managers who offered me support and guidance the following year. With their help, I offered three well-defined resolutions to improve corporate governance and shareholder value, including proposals for confidential voting, a minimum retirement age for directors, and a share repurchase program. I also filed with the SEC (another learning process) and solicited a contesting proxy to elect myself and several others to the board. The response was much the same, muted support though in higher numbers (up to 18% for some measures). I was especially gratified to receive the vote of Institutional Shareholder Services (ISS), the largest independent proxy voting service, which votes proxies for most institutional fund managers.

In a second suit, now pending in Ohio Common Pleas, I sued to obtain the books and records of the bank, which are accessible to shareholders under the same statute that provides access to a list of shareholders. With this suit, I aim to publicly uncover consultants' reports sponsored by the bank over the past decade that recommend improvements in efficiency and capitalization, or a sale of the bank, but which management and the board have ignored. The novel element of this suit is my contention that the bank, nominally a subsidiary of the bank holding company, should be treated by the court as the same entity because the holding company owns no other assets than the bank, owns it wholly, shares the same board of directors with it, conducts its board meetings immediately following the bank's, and occupies the same business address. Piercing the corporate veil in this way and for this purpose is established in the case law of neighboring states, but has not yet been addressed by the Ohio Court.

While I may never receive the support of the 50% of shares required to wrest control of the bank from the incumbent board, I consider my efforts to be a great success. They have led to the replacement of the bank's president, the turnover of four board seats, a measurable shift in the board's attitude toward performance, and increased institutional interest in the equity. Most important, by speaking up I created a climate in which many dissatisfied holders were able to join together to assert their interests. Though small in scale, efforts such as these continually affirm that fiduciary duty is not an empty phrase but a meaningful responsibility that must be upheld. The law creates this responsibility, and the law is the last resort to guarantee its execution.

My goal is to continue to work for shareholders' rights on a larger scale, perhaps by drawing on my training as a financial analyst to identify situations where minority shareholders have been abused and deserve better. Although my first efforts have been successful, if I intend to challenge more sophisticated corporations, I know I will require a thorough understanding of the law. As a student, I hope to learn more about fiduciary duty, securities regulation, negotiation, and litigation. Following law school, I'd like to continue this work as a component of operating an investment fund or by joining a conventional law firm; I will learn which over the next three years. Irrespective of the specific path my career takes, I view good corporate governance as a lynchpin for growth and shared prosperity in America and, where it is deficient, I feel an obligation to improve it.

The shareholder's proxy resolutions prepared for this contest are available on the SEC's EDGAR repository at http://edgar.sec.gov under Croghan Bancshares, Inc. The contesting proxy I wrote and submitted is listed under the SEC corporation index key of Danziger, Samuel R (my father).

Sample 26

Accepted at Lewis & Clark College Northwestern School of Law, Gonzaga University School of Law, and Golden Gate University School of Law

The work of an interpreter is often viewed as nothing more than a person translating two different languages so that people can understand each other. However, I did not anticipate that it was through the role of an interpreter that I would have the chance to analyze myself and reaffirm my college decision to pursue law as a career.

My volunteer work consisted of one-on-one case management sessions with a social worker and Qiao, a Chinese woman with limited English skills who was living at Asian Pacific Work Center's transitional housing. During our sessions, Qiao's legal problems consistently demanded our attention. She was in the process of finalizing her divorce and applying for her immigration petition under the Violence Against Women Act. Qiao's attorney worked with another interpreter, Adam, to assist Qiao with her legal proceedings. Throughout this process, Qiao often had difficulty locating Adam, which resulted in miscommunication between the attorney and Qiao. She would have to make several phone calls and leave several messages for Adam before she could contact him and meet her attorney, which meant that her problems and concerns could not be immediately addressed. At times Qiao became so worried about her case that the social worker would have to step in and contact the attorney directly for Qiao to have Qiao's concern addressed right away.

Seeing Qiao go to great lengths just to meet her attorney and handle her legal problems made me reflect on my role as an interpreter and made me want to offer her more assistance than I was able. Although I work as a legal assistant and have experience with immigration law, my capacity to provide more significant assistance was limited. Listening to Qiao talking about her concerns, I saw that the law would ultimately give her protection and independence. It is crucial that Qiao be granted her divorce and immigration petition so that her lack of legal status does not force her to stay with her batterer. Seeing Qiao's situation, I believe that the legal process is the best recourse for people to address the injustices and inequalities they face.

My work as an interpreter became more meaningful as Qiao shared her world with me. She was not scared to live on food stamps and a small amount of cash assistance after she became separated from her husband. Qiao lacked basic communication skills, but still actively went out looking for a job, attended English lessons, and met with her counselor. No matter what trouble she ran into, she always came to her case management session with a positive outlook.

Working with Qiao on such a personal level, I have come to a better understanding of the world surrounding myself and many other immigrants by witnessing the harsh realties that surrounded Qiao. Though I am an immigrant myself, through my parent's hard work I was fortunate enough not to have to face a situation like Qiao's. Understanding her world was important because working with Qiao was often a challenge. Sometimes I acted impatiently towards her when she talked about issues that seemed irrelevant. Only when I stopped and reflected on Qiao's circumstances did I realize my mistake. I am no longer the naive person who wants to help others, but lacks sensitivity to the person's surroundings. I have come away from this experience knowing that I want to continue to help others, especially women and immigrants. My long-term objective is to work with immigrants and women in the areas of immigration and family law. I wish to educate immigrants about their rights and help them gain access and resources to improve their lives.

Although I always had an interest in law as an undergraduate, I was unsure of how my academic interest would extend to the real world. Therefore, after college, I decided to work as a legal assistant to find out whether I really do want to practice law. Although my interest rests primarily in public interest law, working within a private practice gave me a chance to learn about litigation, immigration, real estate, and intellectual property. I am responsible for drafting pleadings, conducting discovery, and drafting and preparing immigration and patent applications. Additionally, my language ability allowed me to facilitate communication between our clients and our firm. I work closely with our clients throughout the litigation process by helping them understand the legal ramifications of each pleading and then addressing their concerns. My work experiences within the different areas of law have convinced me that I have the intellectual ability required to become a successful law student. While I have not started working as a lawyer, I already feel that my work is significant in that I help protect rights and address grievances. My academic interest during college is further confirmed by my work experiences and I am confident that a law degree will allow me to reach my professional goals.

I am confident that the law is the single greatest avenue for me to effect positive changes in the lives of many individuals, given my background and experience. It is time to build on my life experience and education so that I can continue to help others. I possess the intellectual ability, maturity, and passion to meet the demands of a legal education and a professional career. I look forward to the day when I can take the knowledge and skills I acquire in law school and work on behalf of other women and immigrants.

DIVERSITY STATEMENT

Sample 27

Accepted at San Francisco Law School; wait-listed at University of San Francisco School of Law

Viktor E. Frankl said that one's "unique opportunity lies in the way in which he bears his burden." As an African American minority, my uniqueness has been blatantly emphasized and consistently challenged. My abilities are often ignored or obscured by negative stereotyping or ambiguous labels that foster and encourage false perceptions, misconceptions, mistrust, and low expectations. The resulting behavior of the perpetrators is obstructive, abusive, and sometimes meant to terrorize. I have had to find ways to carry my burden, to endure and thrive. My success can be attributed to the education that I received at an early age, lessons that continue to this day.

At 17, I had played the violin for nine years when during a private lesson, my new violin teacher passionately urged me to "show those white boys!" A retired attorney, he had obviously not been accustomed to an African American violinist with my talent, although he had observed that I was one of three African Americans who played in the citywide youth orchestra. The other two were my brothers. When I repeated the teacher's words to my parents, my mother was livid and proceeded to write him a note which said, "My son is playing the violin for three reasons: 1) Because he can; 2) Because he loves the violin; and 3) Because he loves music. Therefore his reward is intrinsic!" My violin teacher wrote back, "Enough said!" My mother had succinctly articulated what she had always shown me about inner strength. It does not depend on gaining the approval of others, but rather derives from the satisfaction of knowing one has done one's best and done a great job. The incident nudged my awareness. Later in my undergraduate studies and in my professional career, these values would be further tested.

As an undergraduate, I faced a daunting task even though I had been a high school honor student, managing to maintain good grades despite peer pressure to experiment with illegal drugs, alcohol, and truancy. I had survived junior high school ridicule when I arrived at school each day with my violin. Tragically, my playing the instrument was viewed as a sign of weakness by many of my classmates, and I often had to fight to keep my instrument as they tried to take it from me. I had also adjusted to my parents' divorce and the isolation that sometimes accompanies an adolescent in a move to a new city. However, despite my academic preparation and my determination, I was unprepared for the demands of a private university.

One of the first in my family to attend college, I was admitted through an affirmative action program where three out of four failed before their junior year. Students who were not a part of this program treated me as though I was intellectually inferior and not worthy of their time. I was excluded from study groups, test preparation groups, and general academic camaraderie. Suffering from poor time management, the inability to control distractions, and a general lack of academic focus, I floundered as I sought to define my sense of worth and academic direction. My grades reflected my struggle. However, I successfully evolved and transformed myself. My record does not show that I took the majority of the classes that comprised my Computational Mathematics major in my final two semesters, eight intensive time-consuming classes in one academic year. It also does not show that among approximately seventy students admitted through the affirmative action program in my freshman year, I was one of four who succeeded and the only one who graduated with that mathematics major that year. At my graduation ceremony, a tough professor, who I had faced in three of my major's required classes, congratulated me on my effort, exclaiming, "You earned it!"

Throughout my professional career as a software engineer, I have been forced to rely on "intrinsic" rewards to temper unfairness and my resulting anger. I worked for a small company where the President described himself as a "redneck," thereby limiting my opportunities. I have been passed over for promotions, which less qualified white engineers received. Sometimes because of an assumption that I sought unchallenging work, I received less desirable assignments. I have managed project teams of software engineers and struggled to meet scheduled goals because white engineers found a black man's supervision difficult. In making technical presentations, I have faced audiences whose initial expressions were those of utter disgust and defiance rather than eager anticipation. I have succeeded in solving critical, complex technical problems when white engineers, who were perceived as being more qualified, had failed. Yet, I was denied the customary recognition and monetary rewards. It is quite difficult to make choices about what to do when one is the recipient of injustice. I avoided taking on the nearly impossible task of proving that the oppression or wrong occurred because I am African American but always had to choose between maintaining my values and integrity by seeking alternative channels for my ambitions or tolerating the abuse to sustain a standard of living for my family.

Both of these choices have meant adhering to the teachings that have made me who I am. The lessons are as important to me as breathing and represent the essence of two of the most important people in my life: my paternal grandmother and grandfather, both long deceased. These two non-complaining people were born and raised in the segregated South and knew what it took to endure and thrive. My grandmother's faith in a Higher Power to inspire the Human Spirit to overcome was as unshakable as her faith in me and my possibilities. My grandfather was hard working, dignified, and principled—truly an honorable man. My father would say, "He was the finest man I have ever known." By example, these dear people taught me the values that imprinted as respect, dignity, preservation of the family, and hard work. Most important, they taught me to have faith in myself, in effect, how to "carry one's burden" and yet thrive. I am strengthened by what they represented and driven by the principles they stood for. My grandmother once stated, "Some kids you just know have the lord's grace and you are one of them. You'll go far and you'll always do your best."

In addition to my debt to my parents and grandparents, I also thank many who have contributed to who I am and how I thrive—my first violin teacher, my elementary school teachers, my high school English and Math teachers, my freshman football coach, and that one tough college professor who congratulated me at my graduation ceremony. I do not believe that anyone can fully succeed (especially an African American) in any worthy endeavor without the assistance of those who believe in his/her worth. Since no matter how well I am prepared, I can't compete if I'm not allowed in the game, I am extremely grateful to those who not only recognize the inequities for African Americans, but have also attempted to open and level the playing fields.

I salute these great humanitarians. Also, I'm as optimistic about America's future as I am about my own future. I believe that one day there will be no clash or distinction between citizenship and culture. I believe that one day one's color will be of no importance. I believe that someday others will describe me as I describe myself—not with the expedient label of "African American," but as a human with great possibilities, one who is challenging himself to the extent of his capabilities. That I not only believe these things in my heart, but also cultivate the opportunity to articulate them as my mother did, makes all the difference. I am fortunate to be able to teach my three children using the lessons that have sustained me. I am pleased as a parent by their eagerness to attend college one day, their appreciation for the discipline that it takes to learn musical instruments, and their realization that the most satisfying reward is knowing that hard work pays off. I often use a quote that has been attributed to the wisdom of the Tao. "A strong man masters others, a wise man masters himself," I tell my children. I also quote an aphorism I once heard. "There are three kinds of people in this world. Those who make things happen, those who watch things happen, and those who wonder what happened. Make things happen for yourself." With these words, I pass on the strength they'll need to fully actualize their potential and to carry the burden of minority standing, should it be necessary.

ADDENDUM

Sample 28

Accepted at Santa Clara University School of Law

My undergraduate GPA, from almost ten years ago, underestimates my potential for success in law school. While at University of California at Berkeley, I worked part time, and my participation in campus organizations was excessive. I started as the Freshman Representative in the Engineering Society of the University of California (ESUC). By my junior year I was the First Vice-President. Each year I chaired a committee for *Engineer's Week*, contributed to the *California Engineer*, and volunteered for several other projects. Additionally, I served as an officer in the student branches of the Association for Computing Machinery (ACM) and Institute of Electronics and Electrical Engineers (IEEE). I later joined a service fraternity and participated in a variety of community service projects. I also tutored elementary school children in downtown Oakland every Saturday morning for two years.

I graduated from Cal in 1995, and my subsequent grades in both degreed and non-degreed programs are better indicators of my capabilities. I earned a Master of Business Administration (MBA) from the University of Southern California (USC) in 2000 with a cumulative GPA of 3.73. I have a 4.0 GPA for engineering classes I took at California State University, Northridge as a non-matriculating student after completing the MBA. Lastly, in the Master of Science in Computer Engineering program at USC, I have a 3.68 GPA. All of this course work was completed while working full time. These most recent academic experiences demonstrate my abilities as a student, as well as my dedication to further education.

TRANSFER ESSAY

Sample 29

Accepted at University of Chicago Law School

The story of my academic life is one of passion lost and passion regained—or perhaps put better, of one passion lost and another found. Well into my undergraduate years I continued to feed a passion for science and medicine. I chose zoology as a major, focusing my studies in neurobiology and spending time during every break from school shadowing doctors in various fields. Two classes left a lasting impression on me. Organic chemistry, in which the instructor, unlike others, emphasized thinking and processing through complex patterns, rather than straight memorization. In the other course, Embryonic Animal Development, the professor brought a social and critical dimension to the study of science and its uses. I began to realize that for me the pursuit of knowledge was exciting only when coupled with an understanding of its effects on society.

As graduation approached, however, my passion to become a doctor seemed to have vanished mysteriously. In what seemed to be a fit of confusion, I took LSATs without preparation and without any real conviction that I wanted to be a lawyer either. Nonetheless, after graduation, I spent a year working at "Major

Law Firm" to see if I could figure out why my instincts told me to take the LSAT and if law school would be a wise choice for me. Yet, even after gaining some experience in the legal world, I was still not completely convinced. Despite that, I took the plunge and applied to law school.

With such a poor beginning, you can imagine my own surprise when, almost from the start, I found the whole process of being in law school exciting. I thrived on the imminent need to be prepared and the anticipation of being called on in class. I found the intense legal discussions with my classmates to be stimulating—a way to further understand the legal concepts being studied. Not surprisingly, what especially delighted me was the whole process of legal reasoning and argumentation. Unlike many of my classmates, it became immediately obvious to me that the important part of answering a legal question is not the conclusion, but rather how the conclusion is reached. Because I was not attached to a particular conclusion, I would often frustrate my classmates when I argued successfully both sides of a dispute.

Too used to being reticent about myself and a career choice, I attributed my first semester grades to a fluke. Only in the second semester did I finally realize that law really clicked for me—and that is when it really got exciting. I looked with even greater anticipation to group studies, where I could argue all night long with my fellow students. My current experience in the Federal District Court with Judge Martinez has been another incredible, eye-opening experience. I have learned that because legal arguments can be made in many ways, much depends on the mind of the lawyer and/or judge, a formidable responsibility not to be taken lightly. I started to understand that my legal education is a powerful tool that can be used to greatly affect others' lives.

Having my passion rekindled has fired me up and I now feel dramatically more motivated and concerned about what I want to do with my life and how I want to go about doing it. Given a still existing interest in medicine and health care, I want to become a lawyer in the health care field. Because the law has the awesome power to affect so many people's lives, I do not want to be just a lawyer, but a good, even great one and I want to go to a law school that will help lead me to the places where I can have the greatest impact. Not only does the University of Chicago Law School offer one of the best legal educations in the country, it attracts students whose minds will challenge and sharpen my own.

Given the ease with which I excelled at DePaul, I know that I can take up the challenge that the University of Chicago offers—and even enjoy it. I pride myself in being personable and easy-going, characteristics that my classmates comment on even as I have skewered their arguments. I hope to bring these two aspects of my personality to good use at Chicago and in practice: the ability to make powerful arguments while putting people at ease because I really care about them.

LETTER OF RECOMMENDATION

Sample 30

Accepted at San Francisco Law School

December 27, 2002

Law School Admission Council
661 Penn Street
P.O. Box 8508
Newtown, PA 18940-8508

To Whom It May Concern:

This letter serves as my statement of support for Isabel Oneida's admission to law school. My name is Tom Marker, and I am currently a Corporate Trainer for Novus Computer Training and an Adjunct Professor in the Computer Information Technology Department at Great Lakes Community College in Racine, Wisconsin. Prior to this, I was a software manager at MSC Electrochemical Systems in Santa Rosita, California, and previous to that position, a software engineer at Brigadier Government Systems (BGS) in Chandler, Arizona. I hold a Bachelors degree in Electrical Engineering from University of Arizona.

I have known of Isabel's talents since 1989 when we both worked together at BGS. I also aggressively recommended her placement at MSC when I was a manager there, and on her first project with the company, I served as her supervisor and teammate. Close enough to assess Isabel's qualities on any project she worked on at MSC, I was aware that others perceived her as an outstanding software engineer. Having worked with Isabel, I have no doubt that she will be an asset to any law school she attends and I am delighted to provide this assessment of her.

Isabel left Advanced Telenetics to help MSC resolve difficult problems on a massive communications program for the Department of Defense that had been 20 years in the making. We felt fortunate to get her because Advanced was known for employing the best technical minds in the telecommunications industry and Isabel's reputation was so good. She had a stellar reputation as an engineer, not only for her technical contributions at a highly-respected company like Advanced, but also because of her work ethic and effective performance history on programs at Brigadier. She was well liked by all who worked with her and was recommended by no less than eight MSC engineers. Personable, confident, and articulate, upon her arrival Isabel did not disappoint. Given the task of finding a software problem that had plagued the system test efforts for six months, Isabel discovered the problem in two weeks. Thorough and dedicated, she had worked well into the night each day even though she was not being paid for the extra time. She chased down the problem despite the comments from skeptics, who felt she had been proceeding in the wrong direction. She fought off critics whose reputation was on the line if she were to find that the problem originated in software that they had created. Once she found the problem, Isabel presented her findings to members of the project and convinced them that she had identified the source of the problem and devised a solution that required the fewest changes and the least amount of impact to the test schedule. Because of the massive complexity of the system, new hires generally took months to familiarize themselves with the intricacies of this system before they were able to make contributions. The manner in which Isabel resolved this problem is an example of how skillful she is when faced with tough situations.

On another project that was just beginning, Isabel was placed in the difficult position of supporting the development of a system that was to be built utilizing software that nobody at MSC had any experience using. She faced a daunting task because she too was unfamiliar with the new software. In the early stages of development, the other engineers and managers began abandoning the project seeking opportunities with start-up firms but Isabel remained committed. She became the sole developer and accepted the responsibility of not only learning how the new software worked but also how to use it to put a system together according to the deadlines set by the customer. Instead of following the trend of software engineers joining start-up companies in search of instant wealth, she chose to commit herself to building this system because successfully doing so would mean more business for the company. It also represented her first chance to put a system together from scratch to completion. The most highly motivated engineer I have met in my 18 years in the industry, Isabel put her enthusiasm for working on difficult tasks to work. She taught herself how to develop the entire solution using software components that she had never encountered before. She had to meet deadlines and milestones and show the customer that progress was being made so that the customer didn't stop the program, and she succeeded. She researched and purchased books to learn what she needed to succeed. She consulted with Internet experts and made highly technical presentations convincing the customer that MSC was well versed in the new software and technology. Her effort here ranks with that of the best engineers at MSC and I believe is a clear indicator that she is capable of applying herself to the academic rigors of law school.

Moreover, once Isabel became involved in the lawsuit concerning her invention, she was quite animated in discussions about the suit and her discovery of her fascination with the law injected new vigor into her life. I remember thinking that she appeared much more interested in her lawsuit than her work at MSC and I didn't think that could be possible. She had always approached her engineering tasks with enthusiasm, but her interest in the law affected her as if she had won the lottery. It became very obvious to me that she had found her life's pursuit.

Isabel is a mature professional of the utmost character as demonstrated by her commitment to the projects she worked on and to her personal life. She has a certain quality about the way she relates to people that makes her a most effective listener and communicator, no matter how much others' backgrounds and ideas differ from hers. She is considerate and sensitive, possesses a great sense of humor, and is good at understanding the attitudes and perspectives of other people. Equally striking is Isabel's decision to forgo her bright future as a software engineer and mathematician to pursue law. In doing so, she is giving up her top-secret security clearance, which is a highly marketable asset excruciatingly difficult to obtain. A sacrifice of this nature is a clear indication of how deeply she is willing to commit herself and how absolutely she feels that a legal career is her calling.

Isabel obviously enhances the diversity of any law school. She is a Native American who has spent the last 18 years growing in a profession, into which few Native Americans have ventured. She has a vast array of experiences to draw from in both her life experience and career development. Her professional accomplishments have at times required an ability to continue despite the fact that her efforts were not well received. When she had to overcome skepticism concerning her abilities, despite her stellar reputation, she never lost her focus and always presented herself as a woman who sought to solve problems. She never comes across as a woman who views the world as defined by racial boundaries, and her effectiveness and ability to relate to people of any background exemplify this. Colleagues sought out her views on a range of issues, not because of her race, but because her views contain depth and common sense. With her maturity, she will certainly bring focus and commitment to both her legal studies and fellow law students.

In short, Isabel has my highest recommendation, and I very much hope that the committee judges her application favorably.

Respectfully,

Tom Marker

WAIT-LIST LETTER

Sample 31

Accepted by University of San Francisco School of Law and Santa Clara University School of Law; wait-listed at Cornell University Law School and University of North Carolina; accepted off wait-list by American University Washington College of Law

Dear Mr. Shively,

I would like to inform you that I have been accepted to American University's School of International Service Masters Program and have placed a deposit to reserve my position. I look forward to a positive decision on my waitlisted application to the Washington College of Law so that I may pursue this dual degree.

The Washington College of Law continues to be my first choice law school. I am confident that I have the academic background for success, unique international experience to contribute to my classmates' learning, intense motivation to pursue my law career, and drive to help the women of Asia.

Through my professional knowledge, volunteer experience, and international exposure, I will be a unique contributor to class discussions. I also have the inter-personal skills and cross-cultural sensitivity to become a lawyer who can effectively relate to diverse groups of people and champion their causes.

I hope to work with organizations such as the Ford Foundation's Beijing Office and CEDAW. I believe the combination of Washington College of Law's pioneering courses along with the complementary training at the School of International Service's Master Program will enable me to further understand how to apply the experience of women in the United States to improve gender equality for women in Asia.

I have risen to many challenges in the past and am certain that I will succeed at the Washington College of Law as well as the School of International Service. I believe my multi-cultural background, unique work experience, and emotional maturity will be an asset to both American University and the legal profession. I look forward to your decision.

Yours Truly,

Parting Thoughts

If you've invested your valuable time and money in this book, it's probably because you know as well as anyone what a law degree can do for your career and your life. You know it can do more than give you world-beating professional skills and an intense learning experience you'll never forget. It can also open doors, change the way you think, and transform your understanding of yourself and the world.

Like anything offering that much value, there are no magic shortcuts into the Promised Land. After helping hundreds of applicants win admission to the world's best professional programs, I can assure you that the essays that will get you in are not those with the best-executed "mantra," the cleverest angle, or even the most polished prose. The essays that succeed do it through honesty, self-knowledge, and effort. The odds of application success are directly proportional to the amount of candid personal insight and time you put into your essays.

Admissions officers recognize sincerity and hard work, and time after time they reward it. So be real, and give each essay the time it needs to really capture who you are. Good luck!

Bibliography

Abraham, Linda. Best Practices for 2005 MBA Admissions (Los Angeles: Accepted.com, 2004).

———. Submit a Stellar Application: 42 Terrific Tips to Help You Get Accepted. (Los Angeles: Accepted.com, 2004).

Cassidy, Carol-June, and S. F. Goldfarb. *Inside the Law Schools* (New York: Plume, 1998).

Castleman, Harry, and Christopher Niewoehner. *Going to Law School?* (New York: John Wiley, 1997).

Chesla, Elizabeth. *Write Better Essays in Just 20 Minutes a Day* (New York: Learning Express, 2000).

Crews, Frederick. *The Random House Handbook*, 6th ed. (New York: McGraw-Hill, 1991).

Curry, Boykin, and Emily Angel Baer. *Essays That Worked for Law Schools*, rev. ed. (New York: Ballantine, 2003).

Danziger, Elizabeth. *Get to the Point* (New York: Three Rivers Press, 2001).

Dowhan, Adrienne, Chris Dowhan, and Dan Kaufman. *Essays That Will Get You into Law School*, 2d ed. (Hauppauge, NY: Barron's, 2003).

Editors of JD Jungle. *The Law School Survival Guide* (Cambridge, MA: Perseus Publishing, 2003).

Epps Jr., Willie J. *How to Get into Harvard Law School* (Chicago: Contemporary Books, 1996).

Estrich, Susan. *How to Get into Law School* (New York: Riverhead Books, 2004).

"Falcon, Atticus." *Planet Law School* (Honolulu: Fine Print Press, 1998).

Hirshman, Linda. *A Woman's Guide to Law School* (New York: Penguin Books, 1999).

Ivey, Anna. *The Ivey Guide to Law School Admissions* (Orlando: Harcourt, 2005).

Lammert-Reeves, Ruth. *Get into Law School: A Strategic Approach* (New York: Simon & Schuster, 2003).

Lermack, Paul. *How to Get into the Right Law School* (Lincolnwood, IL: VGM Career Horizons, 1997).

Margolis, Wendy, ed. *ABA LSAC Official Guide to ABA-Approved Law Schools*, 2005. (Newton, PA: Law School Admissions Council, 2004).

Martinson, Thomas H., and David P. Waldherr. *Getting into Law School Today*, 3rd ed. (New York: Macmillan, 1998).

Miller, Robert H. *Law School Confidential* (New York: St. Martins, 2000).

Montauk, Richard. *How to Get into the Top Law Schools* (Paramus, NJ: Prentice Hall Press, 2004).

Owens, Eric. *Complete Book of Law Schools* (New York: Random House, 2003).

————. *Law Schools Essays That Made a Difference* (New York: Random House, 2003).

Senechal, Diana, and staff of Vault, eds. *The Law School Buzz Book* (New York: Vault Inc., 2004).

Stelzer, Richard J. *How to Write a Winning Personal Statement for Graduate and Professional School* (Lawrenceville, NJ: Thomson Peterson's, 2002).

Stewart, Mark Alan. *Perfect Personal Statements* (Lawrenceville, NJ: Thomson Peterson's, 2002).

Strickland, Rennard. *How to Get into Law School* (New York: Hawthorn, 1974).

Weaver, William G. *Game Plan for Getting into Law School* (Stamford, CT: Peterson's, 2000).

Whitcomb, Susan Britton, *Résumé Magic* (Indianapolis, IN: JIST Works, 1999).

Wright, Carol L. The *Ultimate Guide to Law School Admission* (Center Valley, PA: Marriwell Publishing, 2003).

ABOUT THE AUTHOR

Paul Bodine is the senior editor at Accepted.com, one of the oldest and most successful online admissions consulting services. His clients have consistently earned admission to such elite law schools as Harvard, NYU, Virginia, Duke, Northwestern, Cornell, Georgetown, and Vanderbilt.